Table of Contents

A Letter from Chuck

I'll never forget the day Charissa, our older daughter, came into the world. Cynthia had experienced a particularly difficult pregnancy, complicated by the grief of an earlier miscarriage and by an auto accident that happened soon after we discovered she was expecting. I had spent much of that time on my knees, praying that the baby would arrive safely and in good health. After weeks of bed rest and close monitoring, the day finally arrived, and the doctor let me know Charissa was safe and sound in her mother's arms. With that news, I wept audibly.

As I look back over forty years ago, I realize that the Lord used that experience to prepare me. I was going to be a little girl's daddy, a role that would require a completely different set of skills than those the father of a son needs. Girls need tenderness. They need safety. They need help in developing a voice and encouragement to trust it—something that comes very naturally to boys, who need to be taught to listen. Girls tend to pick up things quicker than boys, so they need less instruction and more emotional care—fewer lectures, more hugs; less talking, more listening. The time I spent in prayer had prepared my heart for our first little girl, cultivating in me the tenderness and attentiveness that would prove invaluable.

Very much as we did with our first son, we also turned to the Scriptures for instruction, promising each other, "Whatever it says, we'll do." I pored over any passage that had anything to do with rearing a daughter—examined it, dissected it, tested it, applied it, adjusted to it, and then tried again. Each principle I discovered became another opportunity to put God's Word to the test. And as I look back, I naturally wish that I had a chance to push the "replay" button and correct some of my mistakes. But generally speaking, I'm pleased. Both daughters are strong in their faith. They aren't perfect, but neither are their parents. They are remarkable women I am proud to call my daughters.

The principles I learned and insights I gained— sometimes later than I had wished—are here in this *LifeMaps* book. Everything is informed by Scripture, and I have done my best to exclude anything that is not of practical value. As you read the material and work through the questions, I encourage you to stay close to God in prayer. Ask Him to make you especially sensitive to the needs of your daughter and supernaturally wise in your leading.

Believe me, you'll need it . . . but He is faithful.

Charles R. Swindoll

At its heart, a map is the distillation of the experience of travelers —— those who have journeyed in the past and recorded their memories in the form of pictures and symbols. The map represents the cumulative wisdom of generations of travelers, put together for the benefit of those now wishing to make that same journey.

To undertake a journey with a map is therefore to rely on the wisdom of the past. It is to benefit from the hard-won knowledge of those who have explored the unknown and braved danger in order to serve those who will follow in their footsteps. Behind the lines and symbols of the map lie countless personal stories —— stories the map itself can never tell. Yet sometimes those stories need to be told, just as the hard-won insights of coping with traveling can encourage, inspire, and assist us.[1]

—Alister E. McGrath

Welcome to LifeMaps

On a journey, the important thing is not speed as much as it is *direction*.

But sometimes heading the right way requires some guidance. Think about it. You would never set out on a long road trip without first making sure you knew which direction to go, right? You'd consult a map. For many people, the journey toward a deeper and more meaningful relationship with God lies along new or unfamiliar ground. They need directions; they need a map. And, even with a map, sometimes you can still get lost. When you do, it's the locals who know best—those who have been down the same roads. That's why this book is designed to be completed in concert with someone else. Wise friends or counselors can encourage us in our spiritual growth and help us avoid pitfalls along our paths.

Using LifeMaps

LifeMaps provides opportunities for individuals to interact with the Bible in different settings and on several levels, depending upon your particular needs or interests. *LifeMaps* also places a tool in the hands of pastors and other Christian leaders, helping them guide others along a journey of spiritual growth through the study and application of the Bible.

For Individuals

You can use *LifeMaps* in your personal devotions to gain God's perspective on a particular area of Christian living. In addition to offering engaging chapters to read, *LifeMaps* can further your journey of spiritual growth with the help of penetrating questions and opportunities for personal application.

LifeMaps can also serve as a first step to healing or resolving an issue that continues to plague you. Read, reflect, answer the questions, and then contact a competent, mature, godly man or woman to discuss the topic as it relates to your personal situation. This individual can be a pastor, a counselor, or even one of our staff here at Insight for Living in the Pastoral Ministries department. (See page 107 for information on how to contact Insight for Living.) This step is an essential part of the journey.

For Pastors and Counselors

LifeMaps is designed to guide individuals through an engaging, in-depth study of the Word of God, freeing you to help them apply the truths in even more specific and personal ways. As a vital first step in the counseling process, each volume lays a solid biblical, theological, and practical foundation upon which you can build. Encouraging individuals to work through the book on their own allows them the time necessary for personal reflection and education while enabling you to target your ministry of personal interaction and discipleship to their particular needs.

For Groups

LifeMaps can serve as a curriculum for home Bible studies, Sunday school classes, and accountability or discipleship groups. Each book in the series contains enough material for group discussion of key questions and noteworthy passages. *LifeMaps* can also foster meaningful interaction for pastors, elders, staff, and Christian leaders during staff devotionals, leadership retreats, or board meetings.

Suggestions for Study

Whether you use *LifeMaps* in a group, in a counseling setting, in the classroom, or for personal study, we trust it will prove to be an invaluable guide as you seek deeper intimacy with God and growth in godliness. In any setting, the following suggestions will make *LifeMaps* more beneficial for you.

- Begin each chapter with prayer, asking God to teach you through His Word and to open your heart to the self-discovery afforded by the questions and text.

- Read the chapters with pen in hand. Underline any thoughts, quotes, or verses that stand out to you. Use the pages provided at the end of each section to record any questions you may have, especially if you plan to meet with others for discussion.

- Have your Bible handy. Throughout chapters two and four, you'll be prompted to read relevant sections of Scripture and answer questions related to the topic.

- As you complete each chapter, close with prayer, asking God to apply the wisdom and principles to your life by His Holy Spirit. Then watch God work! He may bring people and things into your life that will challenge your attitudes and actions. You may gain new insight about the world and your faith. You may find yourself applying this new wisdom in ways you never expected.

May God's Word illumine your path as you begin your journey. We trust that this volume in the *LifeMaps* series will be a trustworthy guide to your learning and to your spiritual growth.

YOU *and* YOUR *Daughter*

Chapter I

The Destructive Woman

The mansion was as impressive as any I had ever seen. From the living room of a house that boasted no less than ten thousand square feet, I looked across the spacious patio area and Olympic-sized swimming pool to see a putting green and, beyond that, the tennis courts. An eight-foot stone wall surrounded the meticulously manicured estate. My friend had developed his business into the largest and most successful in the city, along with four other enterprises that were thriving because of his talents. It seemed everything he touched turned to gold. He and his wife had become millionaires many times over. But the sanctuary our friends took great care to preserve belied the chaos that had invaded their growing family.

My wife, Cynthia, and I sat on the sofa across from these dear people—a wonderful, mid-forties, solidly Christian couple—and enjoyed lots of laughs throughout the evening. As the conversation turned to children, however, the mood turned to somber. The mother glanced at her husband, and then she said something I'll never forget: "I would give everything we have today for our two daughters to be godly young women. Everything." And with that, she put her head in her hands and sobbed.

The older daughter had become very promiscuous, and the younger was quickly following in her footsteps. Graduation from high school seemed unlikely, as her choice in companions led her to drinking and drug abuse. As Cynthia and I sat and cried with our friends, our hearts beat with theirs: "Oh, Lord, please help us to develop our daughters into wise, godly women!"

While prayer is the first place to begin and must accompany everything else we do as parents, prayer is not our only responsibility. The Lord has given us a genuine stake in the spiritual development of our daughters. Our efforts play a crucial role in their development into wise, godly women. He has given us plenty of guidance in His Word. The book of Proverbs describes two types of women using four sets of contrasting portraits:

The Foolish Woman versus
The Wise Woman

The Contentious Woman versus
The Gracious Woman

The Provocative Woman versus
The Virtuous Woman

The Indiscreet Woman versus
The Godly Woman

The purpose of this study is to understand, in a practical way, the characteristics of a destructive woman as opposed to those of a productive woman by examining these four portraits. If we are able to recognize the early signs of these characteristics, we can respond with the appropriate correction or encouragement while our daughters are still young, before they become hardened. If, in fact, your daughter has become destructive to herself and others by her behavior and choices, take heart. All is not lost. You can still play a significant role in the Lord's plan to win back her heart.

First, I will focus on the unpleasant: a detailed description of what I call "the destructive woman." Solomon describes her in great detail, and while the images he uses are ancient, I think you will find them surprisingly relevant. Cultures and contexts change, but people do not.

Then I will concentrate on the positive: "the productive woman." Solomon has a good deal to say about her. He even ends his book of wisdom with a description of this remarkable kind of woman. His words will be our guide as we discover how to cultivate a godly spirit in the young women the Lord has placed in our care.

Please bear with me in the first half of this book. It will be difficult. I dislike focusing on the negative initially, but I believe it to be important for two reasons. First, we need to take seriously the issue of character in young women. If we plot a line through the petty, annoying, and even destructive characteristics we typically tolerate in young girls, it highlights a path to a dreadful destination. The hope that they will naturally outgrow these behaviors is irresponsible. Daughters need to be taught and led. Second, the warning signs appear early, so they should be addressed immediately.

I encourage you to persevere with me through the first section. You will find the second half—a description of our destination and the application—to be very encouraging. The goal of rearing a godly young woman is both attractive and attainable. But our journey must begin with acknowledgement. I doubt very seriously that your daughter looks like the four grotesque portraits that follow; nevertheless, look for these destructive traits in seed form.

The Foolish Woman

The wise woman builds her house,
But the foolish tears it down with her
own hands. (Proverbs 14:1)

To the Hebrew, the term *fool* described someone who's more than merely slow-witted. A similar term in Arabic means "to be thick," as in someone who is so thick-brained that he or she resists the penetration of knowledge.[1] This term implies the idea of stupidity; however, the Hebrew word connotes foolishness as more of a moral problem than an intellectual one. Such a person refuses to receive instruction and remains closed to constructive feedback, largely because she prefers her sin in spite of the self-destructive consequences. She is especially impatient with discipline and will respond with manipulation. The Lord's definition of a foolish person is one who *chooses* to remain corrupt.

A foolish woman is merely the result of a foolish daughter who never entered the process of growth. She was allowed to remain immature as a young girl, so that by the time she reached adulthood, she became a foolish woman—"devoid of wisdom and understanding, with a focus on the evil behaviors which occur in this state."[2]

Take note of the foolish woman's nonsensical, self-destructive choice in Proverbs 14:1. She tears down her own house with her own hands. The term translated as "tears down" also means "to overthrow" or "to destroy."[3] It's usually used to describe a city's walls in the literal sense and to define, figuratively, a ruler's regime. Tear down a city's walls, and you have overthrown it. It's an act of war or rebellion. When a conqueror overthrows a city, he kills the old authority and steals anything of value he can find. No ruler in his right mind would overthrow his own city.

4

The word *house* means more than just the physical structure. In the Old Testament, a house represented the family and, more significantly, the family's legacy—the wealth and the social standing of future generations. A foolish woman despises everything that does not feed her own self-indulgent appetite. Nothing is sacred to her. She values nothing, not even her own husband, children, or future generations. A woman who overthrows her own household and destroys her own family's legacy is angry and rebellious.

Proverbs 20:11–12 tells us how we can know if a daughter is potentially foolish.

> It is by [her] deeds that a [girl] distin-
>   guishes [herself]
> If [her] conduct is pure and right.
> The hearing ear and the seeing eye,
> The LORD has made both of them.

The term behind the phrase "distinguishes [herself]" means, literally, "to make known," and the word *deeds* could be translated as "daily practice."[4] A daughter tells us who she is through her actions—behavior that follows a distinct pattern. We discover that when a certain kind of event happens, she will react in a certain manner. We can almost predict her response—if we are careful to observe her.

So what are the telltale signs of a foolish girl? I find at least four prominent traits in the book of Proverbs.

Drama

> The woman of folly is boisterous,
> She is naive and knows nothing.
>   (Proverbs 9:13)

Does *boisterous* mean "full of energy"? If so, then nearly all children are foolish! I admire people who have lots of energy and a hearty appetite for activity. Enthusiasm for life is something we should encourage. A better translation of this Hebrew term might be "tumultuous," describing someone who is in constant internal commotion or turbulence.[5] The foolish girl is a drama queen. Her reactions are disproportionate to the routine difficulties she faces. She's continually restless, dissatisfied, fearful, or offended. And if nothing feeds her turmoil, she looks for a way to create it.

Deceit

> The wisdom of the sensible is to under-
>   stand [her] way,
> But the foolishness of fools is deceit.
> (Proverbs 14:8)

Another sign of a foolish daughter is deception. She masterfully twists the truth. She's able to tell you point-blank, eye-to-eye, that such and such is taking place when, all the while, behind the scenes, quite the opposite is true.

Note how the wise woman is contrasted with the liar. The wise woman wants to understand her way—her characteristic manner—while the foolish woman covers her tracks with lies. A wise person takes the time to analyze his or her mistakes, asking the questions, "Now, why did I choose to do that? What triggered my reaction? What circumstances led to my choice?" The wise woman desires to know herself so that she can take command of her life and escape the automatic, thoughtless reactions that cause difficulty and pain later on.

Some time ago, we allowed a young woman from another state to stay in our home. She was pregnant, single, and needed help. After she delivered the baby and placed him in a good adoptive home, we agreed that she should stay with us for further discipleship and preparation for life. But we soon learned that we could not trust her, even in the simplest of matters. When she did something wrong or chose poorly, she avoided taking responsibility by lying.

We had no desire to condemn or reject the young woman. Our desire was to provide a safe, grace-filled environment where she could own her mistakes and examine her behavior, in order to understand her ways and make better choices in the future. But truth often proves too difficult for fools to approach. Truth requires bravery and hard work. And foolish girls prefer the easy way out: deception.

Insolence

> "Stolen water is sweet;
> And bread eaten in secret is pleasant."
> (Proverbs 9:17)

A third sign of a foolish daughter is her mockery of sin and her general insensitivity to guilt. She has a thick, calloused conscience. She lives for the present and ignores tomorrow, and her conscience hardens a little more with each sinful choice.

We had the young lady who was living in our home analyzed by a professional Christian psychologist before making the final decision to have her return to her home state. He told us the young woman could easily become a prostitute because she had the ability, through her dullness toward God and through her insensitive spirit, to carry out the worst sins without the slightest twinge of guilt. She had developed the ability, in her brief twenty years on earth, to do wrong and deceive her own conscience with no effort. Her ability to deceive others gave her the ability to deceive herself, so that wrongdoing became her way of life. And she enjoyed it.

She was a fool who mocked sin. She remained convinced that she could stay one step ahead of the consequences even as they closed in around her.

Antagonism

> Keeping away from strife is an honor for
> a [woman],
> But any fool will quarrel. (Proverbs 20:3)

The Hebrew term translated as "quarrel" means, literally, "to disclose oneself . . . to break out (in contention)."[6] This describes someone who cannot be approached with anything unpleasant, especially if it's personal. She fights back instead of listening. She argues instead of seeking to understand. She's defensive. Furthermore, if a fight doesn't come to her, she looks for one. Few conversations end without someone feeling exhausted by the encounter.

Some people also have difficulty forming relationships in the absence of a conflict. They bond with others by becoming their allies in a fight against someone or something else. If a conflict doesn't exist, they'll fan the embers of some small issue into a bonfire, just to create a reason for deeper interaction. Thriving on chaos, they begin to see the entire world in terms of conflict, pitting one side against the other.

Think about your daughter. Is she in constant turbulence, nursing a negative attitude, and filled with uneasiness and commotion? Are her relationships ultra-dramatic? Is she deceptive? Does she lie or hold back the whole story? Does she think her sins are cute or funny? Is she quarrelsome, defensive, and argumentative?

Don't accept society's opinion or rest in the faulty assurance, "Those are just normal characteristics of growing up." No, these are not traits we would expect in a well-adjusted girl. These are the characteristics of a person who is controlled by the flesh, who is bent on foolishness. Leave your daughter alone, allow her to continue on that same path, and you will release her into a destructive future.

The Contentious Woman

A foolish son is destruction to his father,
And the contentions of a wife are a
    constant dripping. (Proverbs 19:13)

It is better to live in a corner of a roof
Than in a house shared with a conten-
    tious woman. (21:9)

It is better to live in a desert land
Than with a contentious and vexing
    woman. (21:19)

A constant dripping on a day of
    steady rain
And a contentious woman are alike;
He who would restrain her restrains
    the wind,
And grasps oil with his right hand.
    (27:15–16)

I admit some of these are humorous at first glance. However, the laughter fades among those who live in these circumstances throughout their daily existence. Few environments can rob someone of joy like the daily gnawing of a contentious mate, male or female. It just so happens that our current focus is women.

The term rendered "contentious" comes from a root word that "refers to the action of forcibly driving or pushing something away."[7] Usually the term is used to describe someone or something in the act of scattering sheep, such as lions or rustlers. It is also indicative of a person who is not merely argumentative but who drives a wedge between herself and others. Furthermore, she is a divider of people rather than someone who reconciles relationships and encourages peace. She enjoys verbal fights and encourages others to fight. She incites conflict in groups, whether with her family, her coworkers, or her church community. Ironically, she uses conflict to create bonds with people. Her way of relating is by creating enemies and allies.

A woman once wanted my input on a situation but conveyed the story in a way that would have me agree with her viewpoint. She was absolutely determined to have me agree with her, which would have put me on her side of an issue against another party. My reluctance to agree only encouraged her to work harder. Despite my resistance, she stayed on her point . . . and on it . . . and on it! Finally, I had to say, rather firmly, "I am not going to change my position. I do not agree with you." So she stood up, gathered her things, and stomped out.

Now that's a good picture of what these proverbs call "contentious": an argumentative spirit that creates division and drives people apart. This may not be the intent of the contentious woman, but fractured relationships are usually the result.

Some of the signs of a contentious daughter are obvious—but not all.

A Stubborn Will

A contentious daughter cannot (or will not) submit to anyone or anything; not to her parents, not to a legitimate authority, not even to truth itself. Her will is supreme, and her perspective serves her cause. In the place of a sweet, agreeable spirit, a strong, stubborn streak holds her hostage. She has never had her will brought into submission by a loving authority.

Notice, however, I didn't say "she has never had her *spirit* broken." The purpose of discipline is not to break the spirit of a child or to destroy her passion to live life at full throttle. But a child who has been adequately prepared for life in the real world will understand that she cannot always have her way. She must use discernment to know when to stop trying to enforce her will and when to negotiate something reasonable, particularly in relation to others. But if she has always gotten her way or has never had her *will* brought into submission, then she will eventually drive everyone she loves into the desert or to the corner of a rooftop. Her contentiousness will leave her bitter and lonely.

A Spirit of Entitlement

Indulged children become adults with a self-centered spirit of entitlement. They learn that getting what they want comes merely by asking—or begging or manipulating—so that they never learn self-restraint or understand boundaries. If everything they enjoy comes to them at no personal cost, how can they learn the difference between needs and wants? They come to see themselves as deserving everything. To the spoiled daughter, the word *no* is a challenge to be overcome by any means, regardless of the pain of inconvenience.

Now, I have to admit that I found it much easier to say no to my sons than to my daughters. As a father of two boys, I wanted to lovingly make them tough enough to stand on their own as men, be independent, accept limitations, and be eager to work hard for what they may need or want. That made sense in my role as the leader of two young men. But denying my girls anything worked against what I saw as my role—to be their provider and protector. As much as I wanted to shower them with any luxury and any convenience I could afford, I knew this to be something *I* wanted, not what

11

was best for my two girls. I needed Cynthia to hold me accountable, to keep me from thinking too much with my heart. I've come to realize that emotions are wonderful servants, but they are terrible masters.

The contentious woman takes the word *no* as an affront to her rights and an insult to her worth. If she was reared in an overindulgent home and not allowed to see the trade-off between an abundance of material possessions and the necessity of sacrifice, she will not understand the difference between what she wants and what is best.

A Sheltered Perspective

I will also admit that I found it easier to allow my boys to suffer the consequences of their own choices than my girls. Nevertheless, a daughter who is too quickly rescued from the predicaments she creates will have a stunted maturity. She will fail to learn to accept responsibility for the negative consequences stemming from her unwise, selfish choices. She will lay blame at the feet of everyone in her life before acknowledging that her suffering is her own fault. She will fight to the bitter end with anyone who doesn't accept the blame that she, in fact, deserves.

The Provocative Woman

Strange woman is used in the book of Proverbs frequently with reference to a girl who has become promiscuous or overtly sensuous. *Strange woman* is often translated as "adulteress," "foreigner," or "harlot" and comes from a Hebrew term meaning to "be a stranger."[8] It frequently describes someone separated from her normal surroundings. In other words, a "strange woman" has alienated herself or separated herself from her home, her family, or her proper moral boundaries. She is called "strange" because a Hebrew woman who put herself on the street to make her living forfeited the right to be called an Israelite. She became, as it were, a foreigner (a "stranger") to her nation.

The *strange woman*'s prominence in the book of Proverbs stems from the devastating effect she has on others. Take note of how she is described:

> [Wisdom will] deliver you from the
>   strange woman,
> From the adulteress who flatters with
>   her words;
> That leaves the companion of her youth
> And forgets the covenant of her God.
>   (Proverbs 2:16–17)

> For the lips of an adulteress drip honey
> And smoother than oil is her speech. . . .
> She does not ponder the path of life;
> Her ways are unstable, she does not
>   know it. (5:3, 6)

> To keep you from the evil woman,
> From the smooth tongue of the
>   adulteress.
> Do not desire her beauty in your heart,
> Nor let her capture you with her eyelids.
>   (6:24–25)

Notice in each of these verses the role that speech plays in the life of the strange woman. In Proverbs 7:5–21, Solomon explains to his son how to recognize a provocative woman by observing her actions. His descriptive words are amazingly relevant.

> [Wisdom and understanding will] keep
>   you from an adulteress,
> From the foreigner who flatters with
>   her words.

For at the window of my house
I looked out through my lattice,
And I saw among the naive,
And discerned among the youths
A young man lacking sense,
Passing through the street near her
    corner;
And he takes the way to her house,
In the twilight, in the evening,
In the middle of the night and in the
    darkness.
And behold, a woman comes to meet him,
Dressed as a harlot and cunning of
    heart.
She is boisterous and rebellious,
Her feet do not remain at home;
She is now in the streets, now in the
    squares,
And lurks by every corner.
So she seizes him and kisses him
And with a brazen face she says to him:
"I was due to offer peace offerings;
Today I have paid my vows.
Therefore I have come out to meet you,
To seek your presence earnestly, and I
    have found you.
I have spread my couch with coverings,
With colored linens of Egypt.
I have sprinkled my bed
With myrrh, aloes and cinnamon.
Come, let us drink our fill of love until
    morning;
Let us delight ourselves with caresses.
For my husband is not at home,
He has gone on a long journey;
He has taken a bag of money with him,

At the full moon he will come home."
With her many persuasions she
    entices him;
With her flattering lips she seduces him.

I find in these passages no less than five characteristics of a provocative woman. My suggestions to
all parents: Be on the alert for the beginnings of these
in your daughter. However, I don't want to turn you
into an alarmist. Some of these behaviors are bound to
come and go in the life of every young woman. Harping
on isolated occurrences or exaggerating them out of
proportion could actually encourage the very behavior
you wish to address! Our role as parents is to use these
signals as opportunities to instruct our daughters
appropriately, without suspicion, condemnation, or
accusation.

Flirtatious Speech

This is a classic example of something that most young
girls do as they're growing up. It by no means suggests
that a flirt is on her way to becoming a promiscuous
woman. Some flirting is quite innocent, merely conveying interest. However, it is a mark of immaturity, a silly
stage that godly, wise women leave behind. A flirtatious
woman, especially if she is married, is nearly always
an insecure woman. Take note of how the harlot uses
words: "[She] flatters with her words. . . . She seizes
him and kisses him. . . . 'I have come out to meet you,
to seek your presence earnestly. . . . Let us drink our fill
of love. . . .' With her flattering lips she seduces him"
(Proverbs 7:5, 13, 15, 18, 21).

Flirting plays upon the vanity of a man and overtly
communicates the woman's romantic or sexual interest.
It's a tool of seduction. Very often, the girl doesn't intend
for the encounter to become anything more than a

game. In fact, as soon as the boy returns her interest and begins the pursuit, she has the validation she was seeking and often turns her interest elsewhere. There isn't a high school in America where this game isn't played.

However, flirting can become a dangerous game of brinkmanship. Foolish women rarely understand the power of flirting and the effect of flattery upon vain men—especially those men who lack restraint. Neither are they particularly aware of how far they can press the game without taking a moral tumble. Far too often, flirting leads to moral disaster.

Bottom line: don't overreact to flirting, but don't ignore it, either. A father can be the best kind of influence on his daughter in this area. As she begins to mature, he can teach her how to communicate with boys. Words, and how they are used, can mean a great deal to a man in ways that wouldn't register with a woman. A father can translate and reflect his impressions for his daughter in the safety of a nonsexual relationship, so that she can understand how to be kind and affirming with boys without sending a sensual message. Without saying so, a daughter depends upon her father to give her insight into how boys think and are likely to respond.

Alienation from Friends

Proverbs 2:17 describes the strange woman as one who "leaves the companion of her youth / And forgets the covenant of her God." The "companion" in this verse is her husband, and the "covenant" could be either the covenant of Moses, by which she relates to the Lord, or the marriage covenant. In any case, the characteristic is separation. If a daughter suddenly drops her old friends, especially as she begins to blossom physically, parents need to become acquainted with her new friends. If she makes big changes in her activities and the places she goes to have fun, parents need to know what occupies her time and where she spends it. If the new friends are older and the new lifestyle more advanced, there is even more reason to be concerned.

Remember, though, these grown-up changes aren't the problem; they are only symptoms. This is a signal to draw closer to her and discover more about what's going on inside. You may need to restrict her freedom, but only after first taking the time to discover what's happening in her inner life.

Estrangement from God

The strange woman also distances herself from anything that activates her conscience. The last thing she wants is an external reminder of what she's trying to ignore within. Girls taking their first steps down the path of promiscuity usually withdraw from involvement with Christian friends and church activities. They also tend to renege on promises they earlier made to the Lord.

After a woman becomes promiscuous, she will become contemptuous of the very values she once lived out so well for so long. Again, her estrangement is a symptom, not the problem.

Provocative Dress

In Proverbs 7:10, the provocative woman "comes to meet him, / Dressed as a harlot and cunning of heart." The wardrobe of a woman wanting to appeal to a man's darker nature is strategic. And certain articles are so overt they virtually "announce" a woman as promiscuous.

Clothing choices probably present one of the greatest battleground issues between parents and daughters. Our society has legitimized and glamorized sexual impurity, and the fashion industry has long been the lackey of the sexual revolution. So for teens, this some-times means having to choose between being "in style" and being modest in their dress. Equipping a young woman to make good clothing decisions starts *years* before she needs her first bra. I'll explain more about this in the chapter on the productive woman.

The question of modesty changes with the times. In the days of Queen Victoria, catching a glimpse of a woman's ankle was enough to send a man into orbit. Now, outer garments look more like undergarments. Sometimes that's what they are! Furthermore, standards change not only with time but with geography. So I'm not about to start suggesting "appropriate" hemlines or fabrics or styles. However, all clothing is designed to accentuate something or conceal something—to draw the eye to one place over another. When evaluating an outfit, a primary question should be, "What will a young man see *first*?" Another question I recommend that we teach our daughters to ask is, "What does this outfit communicate to men about me?" Unfortunately, many Christian girls and women send the bold message, "I'm available for sex."

Sound harsh? Trust me, it's true. That may not be the intended message, but it's the implication men immediately receive. Let's face it: a tight, low-cut sweater doesn't say, "Please notice my blue eyes." It invites a man to think of the woman as a sex object—a potential partner for physical intimacy. Over the years, men pursuing a lifestyle of purity have to train themselves to keep their eyes and their minds where they belong, and they struggle deeply with women who make it difficult.

Fathers, you especially have to take the lead on this issue. Allow your daughter's mother to stay out of the line of fire. Help to preserve her place as your daughter's shopping companion without spoiling the fun they might otherwise have together. Be the "bad guy." Be the "Neanderthal who knows nothing about fashion." However, please be reasonable! Don't be a prude. But if something clearly crosses a line, say so kindly, quietly, and with the utmost *calm*.

A Wanton Attitude

A wanton, reckless attitude toward life, relationships, and sexuality could be mistaken for healthy exuberance. Much of the modern feminist movement has certainly opened that door. But truth be told, some very destructive attitudes underlie this aspect of a provocative, promiscuous woman.

Many years ago, I was in an airport waiting for my departure, and I decided to browse the book rack. Though I wasn't personally looking for that book, I noticed they had sold out of one particular title on the subject of female sensuality. As I continued to browse the wall for another thirty minutes or so, three women asked the clerk if she had any more in the stockroom. Curious, I asked the young lady behind the counter if she knew anything about it. She said, "Oh, yes. The book is about the science of seduction."

"What do you mean by that?" I asked.

She replied in a cheerful tone, "Well, it spells out in a one-two-three fashion the steps involved in attracting a man."

"You mean attracting him physically?"

She gave me an odd look. "Yeah. Is there any other way?"

I tried to suppress a laugh. "Yes, as a matter of fact. There is."

I later discovered that the book was a national best-seller meant to teach women the step-by-step processes of seducing a man. Since then, dozens have taken its place to articulate a paint-by-numbers process for appealing to the physical aspect of a man, explaining specifically how a woman can control the pace and direction of the relationship using her sexuality.

This is precisely what Proverbs 7:11 means by "She is boisterous and rebellious." Here, again, is the same word we learned earlier. She is "tumultuous"—a woman who is driven by constant internal commotion. She is an emotional thrill-seeker. She is also "rebellious," which one lexicon defines: to "be stubborn, be defiant, be obstinate, . . . i.e., not be willing to change a behavior in any regard, with a feature that the current behavior is in open defiance to authority." [9] This is not a sexually powerful woman impelled by an unquenchable thirst for life. That popular image is a myth. This is a woman ruled by internal forces she cannot comprehend and refuses to analyze. She is moving forward sexually with abandon.

Years ago I discussed this at length with a seasoned, tenured professor at Biola University's Rosemead School of Psychology. I asked him the simple question, "What causes a girl to become promiscuous?" Even though the issue is extremely complex, he was able to point to a few common factors.

He said, "Well, Chuck, it's hard to boil it down. But a number of surveys and studies reveal that if a girl has not received genuine, healthy love from her father—if he was neglectful or voluntarily absent—the girl often tends to blame herself and fills the void by giving herself freely to any man who might give her what dad did not."

"Another common cause," he said, "is sexual abuse. At a very early age, abuse teaches her this very important boundary has little or no meaning. This results in a fear, a distrust, or sometimes a hatred for men. She learns to manipulate a man using her body to get and keep what she needs. By making herself appealing to men by means of unrestrained sensuality or very aggressive sexuality, she, in her mind, controls her destiny. Ironically, this kind of woman finds herself victimized and abandoned over and over again."

"So," I asked, "what would best help a girl avoid this trap?"

He replied, "She needs warmth, love, and healthy physical affection from her father on a regular basis. For example, my daughter and I have a wonderful relationship. One day, she came running up to me on the campus and hugged me, and I held her close in return. One of her friends said, 'Hey, you've got it made. Not everyone can hug a Biola faculty member!'"

That professor's wise psychological advice is also just good, common sense. For promiscuous women, the line between healthy affection and sexual engagement has been blurred. A virtuous woman was given plenty of physical affection by a man who respected those boundaries. It should stand to reason that a healthy woman will know whether a man is loving her or exploiting her. And she respects herself enough to maintain her high moral values.

The Indiscreet Woman

> As a ring of gold in a swine's snout
> So is a beautiful woman who lacks
> discretion. (Proverbs 11:22)

This is commonly known as a comparative proverb. This proverb places a familiar, vivid image alongside a fresh, real-life concept in order to give the reader new understanding. Here we have an object of beauty, "a ring of gold," which corresponds to the beauty of a woman. And we have something repulsive overshadowing that beauty. A pig's snout and a woman's indiscretion are very ugly, no matter how you adorn them.

The word translated as "discretion" means literally "to taste." Figuratively, it refers to the ability to examine and judge something correctly. I like how the NET Bible's notes describe the term:

> The term can refer to physical taste
> (Exod 16:31), intellectual discretion
> (1 Sam 25:33), or ethical judgment
> (Ps 119:66). Here it probably means that
> she has no moral sensibility, no propri-
> ety, no good taste — she is unchaste.
> Her beauty will be put to wrong uses.[10]

We could call an indiscreet woman "shallow." She lacks depth, she fails to apply discernment and insight. The meaning of the word *appropriate* escapes her grasp, and in order to conceal her lack of common sense and reasonable perception, she works on her external beauty. She is insensitive within, unaware, out of touch with reality, gullible, and sometimes naive.

Hope for Tomorrow

What a terrible portrait of a tragic life. I wish I could say that the destructive woman is a rare sight, but she is not. In my role as pastor, I see the best and worst of womanhood and, unfortunately, the trend is not good. That's the bad news. The good news, however, is that the remedy is remarkably simple — costly, but simple.

In chapter three I will describe the productive woman. She is wise, gracious, virtuous, and godly. Invest yourself as a wise parent, and she can be your daughter.

My Questions and Thoughts

My Questions and Thoughts

Chapter 2

The Constructive Parent

You Are Here

The portrait of the destructive woman is distressing to examine as a concept and even more painful to meet in the flesh. You have, no doubt, met her more than once in your travels—and the thought of your daughter becoming like her is intolerable. But we must accept the unhappy fact that from birth every child carries the disease of a sinful nature and, without proper guidance, every girl has the potential to grow up to become a destructive woman.

Fortunately, the Lord has given your daughter a great gift that can help her avoid this awful fate. He has given her you!

The characteristics of the destructive woman appear early in life, but rather than fearing them as deadly trends to quash, we can accept them as opportunities to cultivate wisdom. To help determine where to begin, reflect on how the following negative tendencies are reflected in your daughter.

Which of these specific behavior(s) have you noticed? How do they manifest themselves in her life?

Drama: the tendency to be overly affected by normal trials and tribulations or to be dependent upon or motivated by the upheaval of constant emotional crisis.

_____

_____

_____

_____

_____

Deceit: an unwillingness to accept responsibility for her own emotions and actions, usually manifested by blaming others or concealing the truth.

_____

_____

_____

_____

_____

Insolence: a passive-aggressive hostility toward authority figures or resentful attitudes and actions toward authority in general.

_____

_____

_____

_____

_____

Antagonism: the tendency to bond with others by creating allies in a conflict that she either creates or seeks out, or the continual instigation of conflict.

_____

_____

_____

_____

_____

Provocativeness: a preoccupation with boys, an inability to feel affirmed, secure, or self-assured without a steady boyfriend or the attention of the opposite sex.

_____

_____

_____

_____

_____

Many of these characteristics are typical of normal childhood because they describe immaturity. Normal children are immature. Our role as parents is to ensure that they don't remain that way. On the other hand, in rare cases, these characteristics may point to a very serious psychological or emotional problem, as the following example illustrates.

Soon after Kim's thirteenth birthday, she began behaving very differently. She had been a good student, interested in her grades, and active in sports. She had been excited about activities with her youth group and enjoyed going to church. She and her parents tussled over household chores, homework, and getting along with siblings. Nevertheless, she was typically affection-ate and generally connected to the family. She wasn't the ideal daughter. She was normal. But this quickly eroded after she and a boy at church became a couple—at least in the wobbly, junior-high sense of the word. Grades declined, and TV-watching escalated. Kim dropped out of volleyball, begrudgingly went to church, rarely left her room, and became belligerent about almost everything.

Kim's parents did what any conscientious parents would do. They met each behavioral challenge with a clear statement of the problem along with appropriate consequences, which resulted in her privileges and freedoms gradually disappearing over a four-week period. Kim's parents applied the same parenting strategies that had helped her become the well-adjusted teenager she had been only a few weeks before. But discipline only fueled her rebellion.

Finally, Kim's dad took her to a trained Christian psychologist who helped adolescent girls as the primary focus of her practice. After a couple of sessions, Kim revealed that her boyfriend had coerced her into having sex. Suddenly, everything made sense. A deadly concoc-tion of guilt, shame, disappointment with herself, fear of God's judgment, fear of pregnancy, the need for male attention, and continued pressure from the boy had poisoned Kim's spirit. She was wasting away, and her difficulties were far more serious than most parents are equipped to address.

A sudden and dramatic shift in behavior over a few weeks is not normal. Something significant has occurred, and it is not likely that routine parental involvement will be enough. This *LifeMaps* book is not intended to substitute for medical care in the case of mental illness or competent counseling in the case of serious emotional difficulties. Don't hesitate to ask for assistance, and don't think that making a call suggests you are a failure as a parent. Just as some physical illnesses require help from a doctor or hospital, some behavioral problems will need the help of a professional who is both spiritually astute and trained in psychology.

If, on the other hand, you have seen the negative qualities of the destructive woman at work for some time, this is your opportunity to help your daughter grow.

 ## Discovering the Way

An encounter with foolishness should always lead us to examine Scripture, our only reliable source of absolute truth. Carefully observe each of the following passages, looking for a timeless principle that will guide your parenting. It will be helpful to review the corresponding sections in the previous chapter as you study each passage.

Drama

> The woman of folly is boisterous,
> She is naive and knows nothing.
>   (Proverbs 9:13)

The first line makes a statement about the foolish woman, while the second explains it. Why is the woman "boisterous" (in other words, tumultuous, disquieted)?

_____

_____

_____

_____

_____

In Hebrew, the verb form of the word translated as "naive" means to "'be open, spacious, wide,' and might relate to the immature or simple one who is open to all kinds of enticement, not having developed a discriminating judgment as to what is right or wrong." [1]

In a practical sense, what does naïveté look like in the life of a foolish woman? List specific behaviors or attitudes.

_____

_____

_____

_____

_____

Given the above definition of _naive_, what vital knowledge does the woman in Proverbs 9:13 lack?

_____

_____

_____

_____

_____

What is the remedy for naïveté and "knowing nothing" (Proverbs 1:2–9; 8:5–11)?

_____

_____

_____

_____

_____

How does the quality of discernment influence a person's response to life and its inevitable difficulties?

_____

_____

_____

_____

_____

Deceit

> The wisdom of the sensible is to under-
>   stand [her] way,
> But the foolishness of fools is deceit.
>   (Proverbs 14:8)

The Hebrew language uses four terms to quantify the level of foolishness in a person. Each successive term includes and builds upon the qualities of the previous one. Note that the greatest fool of all is the person who is intelligent, yet disobedient!

> *Kesil*: Lacking knowledge, mentally
>   sluggish[2]

> *Ewil*: Callous to the moral implications
>   of foolish choices[3]

> *Nabal*: Willfully closed to wisdom and
>   brutishly destructive to self and
>   others[4]

> *Letz*: Incorrigibly and willfully
>   rebellious against God[5]

The two lines of Proverbs 14:8 draw a stark contrast between the "wisdom of the sensible" and the "foolishness (*ewil*) of [the] fools (*kesil*)." In your own words, describe how the wise and foolish differ.

_____

_____

_____

_____

_____

Using this verse as a guide, give a specific example of how a sensible person would respond to being confronted with a personal fault. How would a fool respond?

_____

_____

_____

_____

_____

_____

_____

_____

Insolence

"Stolen water is sweet;
And bread eaten in secret is pleasant."
(Proverbs 9:17)

How would you describe the overall perspective of someone who exhibits the quality described in this proverb?

_____

_____

_____

_____

_____

Now, how does a person with this perspective typically respond to authority?

_____

_____

_____

_____

_____

When faced with rules or expectations, does this person tend to respect and obey them? Why, or why not?

_____

_____

_____

_____

_____

Antagonism

> Keeping away from strife is an honor for
> a [woman],
> But any fool will quarrel. (Proverbs 20:3)

Also read Proverbs 15:18, 17:14, and 19:11.

Why is the foolish person continually in conflict?

_____

_____

_____

_____

_____

Why do you think conflict appears to be easier or feels better than peacemaking to a foolish person?

_____

_____

_____

_____

_____

_____

_____

_____

Provocativeness

Indiscriminant sensuality is reason for grave concern. Read Proverbs 7:5–21 for Solomon's description of the provocative woman's behavior.

Read Proverbs 7:5, 13–18. How does the provocative woman use flirtatious speech to attract a man?

_____

_____

_____

_____

What kind of man would find this enticing?

_____

_____

_____

_____

The word rendered "flatter" comes from a Hebrew term that can be translated "divide" or "be smooth," depending upon the context.[6] When used regarding one's speech, it retains a strong sense of both meanings.

Read Proverbs 7:10. How does the provocative woman adorn herself to attract a man?

_____

_____

_____

_____

Describe a recent fashion trend that you would consider provocative.

_____

_____

_____

_____

What does revealing or provocative attire communicate to men?

_____

_____

_____

_____

Read Proverbs 7:13. How would you describe the provocative woman's behavior in general?

_____

_____

_____

_____

How have you seen teenage girls mimic this behavior? Where do you think they saw or experienced this behavior originally?

_____

_____

_____

_____

Why do you think a woman or a young girl would crave the attention of men she does not know or who are clearly unsuitable?

_____

_____

_____

_____

Starting Your Journey

Proverbs 20:11–12 says, "Even a [woman] is known by [her] actions, by whether [her] conduct is pure and right. Ears that hear and eyes that see—the LORD has made them both" (NIV). Careful observation gives the parent valuable insight so that he or she can provide the right instruction at the right time. Combine your earlier observations with the principles you gleaned from Scripture and plan how you will respond when your daughter behaves foolishly.

Not all of the following issues will accurately describe your daughter. Skip over the ones that do not apply.

Drama

What circumstances typically cause your daughter to become overly emotional or erratic in her behavior?

_____

_____

_____

_____

Do you think calling attention to her overreaction would help or hurt the situation? Why, or why not?

_____

_____

_____

_____

_____

_____

_____

How can you encourage her to think and behave more wisely?

_____

_____

_____

_____

Deceit

Very often deceit is an attempt to avoid accepting responsibility for one's own emotions, attitudes, or choices. In what circumstance(s) is your daughter most likely to bend the truth, either for herself or for others?

_____

_____

_____

_____

How can you create a safe environment for your daughter where she can recognize and accept her own flaws, faults, and mistakes?

_____

_____

_____

_____

How might revealing your own struggles and how you handle them help her?

_____

_____

_____

_____

Insolence

Why do you think your daughter resents authority figures or reacts negatively to rules?

_____

_____

_____

_____

As children approach the age of 10, they begin to make a subtle but profound shift in their thinking. In their childhood years, they took the instruction of parents and other adults at face value. But as they reach early adolescence, they have a growing need to test the integrity of everything. They want to know the reasons for rules, they question the values they once took for granted, and they scrutinize the behavior of role models, looking for discrepancies between what is taught and what is lived.

When your daughter points out a genuine flaw or failing of yours, how do you typically respond?

❏ I change the subject or find a way to distract my daughter.

❏ I point out a similar flaw or failing in my daughter and explain how she can address it.

❏ I help her see how my experience is different from hers and why my actions are not wrong.

❏ I readily admit the flaw or failing and genuinely determine to address it meaningfully.

❏ I am the parent, so I don't allow her to question me or judge my actions.

How might your response have aggravated any resentment your daughter has for authority or standards?

_____

_____

_____

_____

How can you use your life experiences to demonstrate the value of respecting authority and honoring standards of conduct?

_____

_____

_____

_____

_____

_____

_____

Antagonism

Conflict, while unpleasant, can provide a person with some short-term benefits. Righteous anger, for instance, feels powerful and diverts attention from one's personal flaws or failings. Bonds form between people who fight on the same side of a controversy. Arguing the finer points of a disagreement helps a person to avoid the real issues, which may prove him or her wrong. However, the short-term benefits nearly always create deeper, more serious difficulties, especially if these tactics become habitual.

Habitual friction and a persistent spirit of contention usually stem from a fear of being wrong and what that implies about one's worth. Closely connected with this is a fear of being rejected or abandoned. Addressing self-image and security issues will reduce your daughter's need to deny or defend.

What can you do to help your daughter gain a greater sense of her worth?

_____

_____

_____

_____

What role do you think a personal relationship with the Lord can play in this?

_____

_____

_____

_____

Brainstorm some ways you can address failures and faults while affirming your daughter's worth and her place in your heart.

_____

_____

_____

_____

_____

_____

_____

Provocativeness

Helping a daughter grow into her adult body and come to terms with her sexuality is a lifelong process that begins soon after birth. It begins by helping her develop a healthy admiration for how her body reflects God's design, allowing her to feel comfortable in her own skin. At the appropriate age (perhaps 9–12), targeted, topical education will equip her to understand the physical, emotional, and spiritual components of sexual intimacy. Then comes the difficult task of helping her manage her sexuality responsibly as a flood of hormones and peer pressure try to tear her from the moorings you so patiently built.

Stanton and Brenna Jones have written an excellent guidebook titled, *How and When to Tell Your Kids About Sex: A Lifelong Approach to Shaping Your Child's Sexual Character.* This is not a book about sex education; it describes a program for character formation. If, for whatever reason, your daughter was not given this guidance prior to her adolescence, it's not too late to begin, although you will likely have to start from the beginning and work forward. For example, a girl must see her body as valuable first, or the notion that she should take care of it will not make sense. Nevertheless, your daughter will welcome your constructive involvement, even if it's later in her life.

Children are born foolish. They are naive, impetuous, overly emotional, shortsighted, and completely uninhibited. But let's face it; that's part of their charm. That's why we enjoy them so much. However, if they never outgrow their foolishness, it's neither charming nor lovable. They need someone to help them exchange hurtful self-destructive behavior for wise, self-respecting choices. Only then will they learn to serve something outside themselves.

The first half of this book has made the negative qualities of the destructive woman the object of intense scrutiny. It was an unpleasant yet necessary exercise. However, there is much more to learn from the positive traits of the constructive woman. The second half will provide a detailed study of feminine wisdom.

My Questions and Thoughts

Chapter 3

The Productive Woman

After the dismal portraits of the destructive woman, these pages will be a welcome breath of fresh air. In chapter 1, I introduced four sets of contrasting portraits found in the book of Proverbs. In these same portraits, I find sketches of the godly woman we pray our daughters will become as we apply specific principles from God's Word to our parenting. They are:

The Wise Woman versus
The Foolish Woman

The Gracious Woman versus
The Contentious Woman

The Virtuous Woman versus
The Provocative Woman

The Godly Woman versus
The Indiscreet Woman

The Wise Woman

To the Hebrew, wisdom is the exact opposite of foolishness. Just as foolishness encompasses more than mischievousness or a lack of intelligence, wisdom maintains a strong emphasis upon one's will—one's actions, morality, and obedience to God. This definition sets the Hebrew concept of wisdom apart from that of all other cultures. The Greek culture limited wisdom to understanding. Other Near Eastern cultures added practical application to understanding. In other words, if a woman knows something to be true, certainly she would live by it. Hebrew wisdom, however, adds a third all-important dimension: holiness.

The *Theological Wordbook of the Old Testament* describes Hebrew wisdom this way:

> Reflected in OT wisdom is the teaching of a personal God who is holy and just and who expects those who know him to exhibit his character in the many practical affairs of life. This perfect blend of the revealed will of a holy God with the practical human experiences of life is also distinct from the speculative wisdom of the Greeks. The ethical dynamic of Greek philosophy lay in the intellect; if a person had perfect knowledge he could live the good life (Plato). Knowledge was virtue. The emphasis of OT wisdom was that the human will, in the realm of practical matters, was to be subject to divine causes. Therefore, Hebrew wisdom was not theoretical and speculative. It was practical, based on revealed principles of right and wrong, to be lived out in daily life.[1]

When we return to Proverbs, we see how a wise woman differs from the fool.

The wise woman builds her house,
But the foolish tears it down with her
own hands. (Proverbs 14:1)

While the foolish woman is an irresponsible destroyer, the wise woman is a careful builder. The foolish woman is destructive, while the wise woman is constructive. Remember that in ancient cultures, the term *house* meant more than the structure (Joshua 24:15; Ruth 4:12). This proverb isn't suggesting that your daughter needs to learn plumbing or carpentry. The phrase "builds her house" means that a wise woman takes an active, personal interest in her family's well-being and future legacy. Rather than having the contemptuous, selfish attitude of the foolish woman, the wise woman sees herself as part of something greater. She willingly sets aside short-term gratification in favor of what is best for her household. She has a spirit of submission, a balanced view of give and take rather than a selfish spirit of rebellion.

Now, as I emphasized before, the signs of wisdom appear early in life and can be observed in a young girl's daily interactions. Furthermore, wisdom can be cultivated by wise parents. Begin by observing your daughter through the following lens: Is she selfish to the point of ignoring the bigger picture? Does she regard the family and the household as something that exists to meet her needs and satisfy her desires? Or does she recognize that she is an important member of the family and that her contribution is significant?

All children are given to selfish foolishness at times, so don't be alarmed when you occasionally witness that in your daughter. She is young . . . she also has your fallen nature! But you are wise if you remain ready to take appropriate action. According to Proverbs, the path to wisdom begins with discipline. I do not find in the book of Proverbs any counsel that suggests merely talking with a fool. In fact, the Bible says that reasoning with a fool is a waste of time. Instead, Proverbs 22:15 says, "Foolishness is bound up in the heart of a child; / The rod of discipline will remove it far from [her]." Proverbs 29:15 says, "The rod and reproof give wisdom, / But a child who gets [her] own way brings shame to [her] mother." The literal Hebrew behind this proverb is complex, so translators do their best to supply a meaningful interpretation. The latter half of the proverb reads, literally, "but a child *left* brings shame to [her] mother."

"A child left." That doesn't mean that she was left out in the cold or sent to her room or abandoned. The most likely meaning is "left in the condition in which she was born." It's an unusual form of the Hebrew verb that could also be translated "let go" or even "sent away." [2] A child having certain gifts and bents who is delivered into the hands of parents and then left without instruction, training, boundaries, discipline, and direction will ultimately shame them. The picture is one of neglect, lack of concern, or passivity on the part of the parent.

Notice that discipline involves both "the rod" and "reproof." Some expositors would disagree, but I think Solomon had two distinct ideas in mind: the rod, a physical instrument of discipline; and reproof, a verbal correction. A wise parent employs both in order to keep rebellious attitudes in check.

Of course, "the rod" is a visual image of corporal punishment, but it's not limited to that. The bigger idea includes consequences. For younger children, this could be a spanking (not too severe . . . not too long) or a meaningful time-out. For older kids, it could be grounding, removing privileges, or restricting the use of property. The purpose of the rod, whatever form it takes, is to get the message across that "Your actions will have repercussions." Spanking is one form of the rod, but remember, it's not the only one. The purpose of the rod is to establish authority and to seize the child's attention.

"Reproof" is verbal correction, which must *always* accompany punishment. Every application of the rod requires instruction: an explanation of what went wrong, a discussion of why the rod was necessary, an affirmation of the child's value, and always a reminder of how much she is loved. All of this must be done in private. Never, ever discipline a child in public or in front of the family. Nothing is gained by embarrassing a child. In fact, the humiliation will likely drown out any message she might otherwise hear.

The root of the English word *discipline* is "disciple." Reproof, or verbal correction, doesn't always have to be given in response to something negative. In fact, our verbal guidance in the form of encouragement and affirmation should outweigh our reprimands ten to one — Please read that again! If you see your daughter doing something right, however small or insignificant, praise it. She will want more affirmation and will look for opportunities to hear your positive feedback again and again. Ideally, this constant flow of positive input will prepare her to receive your correction later.

In that spirit, Proverbs 31 describes the quintessential wise woman and points to several positive ways we can cultivate wisdom in our daughters.

Affirm Her Worth

> An excellent wife, who can find?
> For her worth is far above jewels.
>> (Proverbs 31:10)

Start early. Call your daughter the very things you hope she will be, and help her realize the value of being wise. Use your life experiences and the things that God has taught you to help her appreciate the rarity and the beauty of a wise woman.

Dads, point to the qualities in your daughter's mother that you appreciate. Be specific. "See how Mommy takes care of others? I love that about her!" "See how she takes time to make our home a peaceful place? She's wonderful!" "Look at Mommy in that outfit! Isn't she elegant? Isn't she beautiful?" Point to other worthy examples in wise women. Help her to understand what wisdom looks like.

Encourage a Serving Attitude

The woman of Proverbs 31 is described as one who devotes herself to the building up of others.

> The heart of her husband trusts in her,
> And he will have no lack of gain.
> She does him good and not evil
> All the days of her life.
>> (Proverbs 31:11–12)

> She rises also while it is still night
> And gives food to her household. (31:15)

> She extends her hand to the poor,
> And she stretches out her hands to the
>> needy. (31:20)

She opens her mouth in wisdom,
And the teaching of kindness is on her
    tongue.
She looks well to the ways of her
    household. (31:26–27)

Teach your daughter the value of investing in the lives of others, particularly within the family. When she contributes to the household by cleaning her room, doing the dishes, or helping with chores in and around the house, praise her. Let her know that her involvement has value to the family. Be sure to point out how everyone benefits because she chose to invest in her family.

Develop Her Talents

As a young, single, Christian man, I worked closely with another bachelor on an evangelistic team, traveling around southwest Texas and parts of Oklahoma and Louisiana. One of the team members was a young man named Jimmy Draper. He was a remarkable young minister among the rest of us girl-crazy teens. We were talking about girls and what we hoped to find in our future mate. He asked me, "Do you know what I look at first on a girl?"

I thought, "Oh, boy. Here we go. Mind in the gutter." How wrong I was!

"I look at her hands."

I was pleasantly surprised but puzzled, so I asked, "Why her hands?"

"Because of Proverbs 31:13."

We grabbed a Bible and found the verse:

"She looks for wool and flax / And works with her hands in delight."

He continued, "I'm amazed by what you can discover about a girl by looking at her hands."

You can tell when someone's hands have been idle. But hands that play an instrument, ply a craft, plant a garden, or carry out responsibilities in other ways belong to a diligent woman with depth. A girl who works to develop a talent she enjoys is, by nature, less vain or self-centered. She enjoys a peaceful confidence and a quiet spirit; she is free of the commotion that churns inside a turbulent, emotionally tumultuous girl. She thrives on peace, not chaos.

Help your daughter discover her God-given talent and encourage her to be industrious with it. If her talent is playing an instrument, encourage her to practice hard and play with confidence. If her talent involves working with her hands, suggest she give whatever she makes to someone who would appreciate it. If you can join her or participate somehow in what she creates, make time to do it together.

Teach Money Management

> She is like merchant ships;
> She brings her food from afar.
>   (Proverbs 31:14)

> She considers a field and buys it;
> From her earnings she plants a
>   vineyard. (31:16)

> She makes linen garments and
>   sells them,
> And supplies belts to the tradesmen.
>   (31:24)

I'm not sure why, but it seems to go without saying that our son should know how to handle money as he becomes a man. Why aren't we as serious about this same issue with our daughters? We love to crack jokes about girls, shopping, and credit cards, but how deliberate are we about teaching them money-management skills? Proverbs 31 describes a very shrewd, business-savvy woman who could hold her own in our modern corporate world. And I suspect she didn't become that way by accident. Someone taught her.

I would suggest giving your daughter an allowance. Make it generous. Then refrain from buying her very much beyond what she needs. Encourage her to use her allowance to buy what she wants. For maximum impact, the amount of her allowance needs to be substantial. Otherwise, she will have no reason to take it seriously. When she asks for something, use the opportunity to review her account. "How much is there?" "Where did it go?" "If you had known earlier that you were going to want this, what would you have done differently with your money?" "How 'bout I help out this time, but next time you save up your money?"

When it's time to go clothes shopping, hand her the cash you would have spent and drive her to the mall. Offer to help, but let her make the decisions. Let her know, "If you spend it all on two pairs of really cool shoes, that's all you're going to have for the next six weeks" (or whatever time period you had in mind). Then let her live with her purchases if she goes against your counsel. I warn you, she'll completely blow it a time or two. Don't be upset. Willingly let her decide and then allow her to live with her decisions. And though it will be difficult, do your best to avoid the "I told you so" reaction or even tone of voice. When she complains about her choices, show her *authentic* sympathy.

As your daughter approaches adulthood, allow her to see more of the family finances, including the foolish decisions and unwise expenditures you've made. Talk honestly about the tough lessons you learned and how you avoid making the same mistakes again. You might even ask her to manage a portion of the family budget, such as groceries. And be sure to warn her about the credit card trap! She may resent you now, but she *will* thank you later.

Encourage Hard Work

> She girds herself with strength
> And makes her arms strong.
> She senses that her gain is good;
> Her lamp does not go out at night.
> (Proverbs 31:17–18)

> Strength and dignity are her clothing,
> And she smiles at the future. (31:25)

> She looks well to the ways of her
>   household,
> And does not eat the bread of idleness.
> (31:27)

Wise women are not idle. As I mentioned earlier, they know the value of hard work. Foolish women wait for someone else to carry their load. By avoiding work, they exchange dignity for dependence. Take note of the phrase, "Strength and dignity are her clothing." The woman of Proverbs 31 is hardworking and industrious.

How long has it been since your daughter's fingernails were dirty? When was the last time she set a goal and then worked hard to achieve it? How seriously does she take her schoolwork? How consistent are you to model and encourage excellence?

You can influence her desire to work hard by your speech and by your example. In your speech, do your best to talk about work in positive ways. Avoid complaining about the boredom, the low pay, the boss, the lazy coworkers, the poor work conditions, the problems, or the stress of your job. If you were a child listening to that every day, why would you want to work? Instead, highlight your accomplishments. Talk about a challenge, what you did to successfully overcome it, and how that made you feel. Let your daughter know that the nice things in your home are the rewards of faithful labor.

Never underestimate the power of your example. Your daughter may not admit it, but she is impressed by you. What you do matters. Invite her to help you with a big chore, and then reward yourselves with a treat. Let her see where you draw a paycheck and what you do. Having finished what you started, allow her to see your satisfaction with a job well-done.

A wise woman is the product of consistent attention and training. Neglect breeds a fool. Do your best to find her doing something well, and then use that opportunity to praise and affirm her. Observe your daughter, and deal with foolish behavior directly and without delay. If you don't, those issues will cause difficulty later on when the stakes become much higher.

I remember one incident where an older teenaged daughter threw her family into a panic with a particular decision she was about to make. She was bent on having her own way. Her father counseled her in one direction and the young man in her life pulled her in another. The anxious dad called me just as I had landed in an airport far from home, so I wasn't able to meet with them right away. But he assured me, "She says whatever you recommend is what she will do, Pastor Swindoll."

Once I heard the details, I responded, "I believe your daughter ought to do exactly as you have said, my friend. And I would like to meet with you, your wife, and your daughter when I return home." So we made arrangements. In the meantime, the girl was true to her word and followed our instructions.

When I returned, we gathered in my study where I had the privilege of presenting a very simple illustration that showed how certain anchors are dropped during childhood. If they are not dealt with, they drag across the bottom. As our boat sails on through life and we get older, the anchor keeps on dragging along, slowing us down until we address the issue.

Before I could finish the illustration, the young lady said, "That's me! I know where it happened!" She didn't elaborate, and I didn't ask. But she said, "I can look back and remember when that happened—when this strong, stubborn streak of mine began." She, her mother, and her father looked at one another, and I could tell they needed nothing more from me. Within a few moments, the young lady had dissolved in tears saying, "For the first time, I see it! I realize how wrong I've been." (I wish all counseling experiences were that successful).

The only downside to that very positive experience was the realization that the issue could have been resolved with much less pain and trauma if only it had been addressed earlier. The cultivation of wisdom occurs bit by bit, day by day, lesson by lesson, week after week. It is the result of calm, faithful training. Consistency is the key.

The Gracious Woman

> A gracious woman attains honor,
> And ruthless men attain riches.
> (Proverbs 11:16)

Graciousness means "to show favor," to show consideration and acceptance.[3] The grace of a woman can be seen in three primary ways.

Her Speech

> She opens her mouth in wisdom,
> And the teaching of kindness is on her
> tongue. (Proverbs 31:26)

Her words are kind. Rather than using her speech to divide people like the contentious woman, she builds bridges of peace with her words. Furthermore, the phrase, "teaching of kindness," could also be translated, "loving instruction."[4] The gracious woman does her best to increase understanding with her kind words rather than forcing her point of view on another through argument.

Her Appearance

> She makes coverings for herself;
> Her clothing is fine linen and purple.
> (Proverbs 31:22)

While the wise woman is industrious, generous, and a good manager of money, she also has exquisite taste. In the ancient world, purple linen was the clothing of royalty. While she understands that "charm is deceitful and beauty is vain," she nonetheless presents herself in an attractive, dignified manner. Unfortunately, many Christians believe that to be godly is to be homely—no makeup, no jewelry, no fine clothing—which is discouraging to many women who have their priorities straight and yet delight in the process of feeling beautiful. The gracious woman doesn't neglect this delightful aspect of femininity.

Many years ago, Anne Ortlund wrote a wonderful book for women titled *Disciplines of the Beautiful Woman*, in which she offers this description of genuine, godly beauty. If we are going to reject Hollywood's idea of beauty, we need to replace it with something. I think this is a worthy model.

> The beautiful woman is disciplined, chaste, discreet, deferring, gracious, controlled, "together." This kind of woman God considers godly, which means she's got his qualities, and she's close to his heart. This is "*his* kind of woman"—his kind of beautiful woman.
>
> Now, under this umbrella of characteristics, she can have all kinds of personalities and still be beautiful. She can be vivacious or shy, colorful or cool, an administrator or a follower. She can be a corporation president or she can bake delicious molasses cookies—or both.
>
> When a woman has God's beauty— a meek and quiet spirit—she isn't threatening to those around her. She doesn't compete; she doesn't "demand her rights," because she's secure. Her trust is in God to exalt her in his own way and time, and he does! He can afford to expand her gifts and increase

her place in the world, because she's
not grasping for it. That's God's kind of
beautiful woman.[5]

Her Attitude

> She does him good and not evil
> All the days of her life. (Proverbs 31:12)

> Her children rise up and bless her;
> Her husband also, and he praises her,
>   saying:
> "Many daughters have done nobly,
> But you excel them all."
>   (Proverbs 31:28–29)

The contentious woman possesses a stubborn will
because she never learned that she cannot always have
her way. Her will was never brought into submission
by a loving authority who set reasonable limits on her
conduct. The gracious woman, on the other hand,
displays a spirit of cooperation and negotiation with
those around her. She respects authority and seeks to
accomplish her will in ways that honor others. As a
result, her attitude earns the respect of her family.

If I had to sum up the qualities of a gracious
woman, I would choose the words *appreciation* and
affection. She knows how to appreciate others, and
everyone returns her good favor. And she's comfortable
showing affection, especially to her children and to her
husband. Godly, gracious women aren't stingy with
hugs, caresses, and kisses for their families.

Young girls learn to be gracious women primarily
from their mother's example. Fathers supplement such
learning by treating their daughters with tenderness and
dignity.

The Virtuous Woman

An excellent wife is the crown of her
husband,
But she who shames him is like rotten-
ness in his bones. (Proverbs 12:4)

The Hebrew word translated as "excellent" literally means "to be firm, to be strong, to be capable and efficient." When used of a good man, it has been rendered "valiant." The qualities we normally associate with a valiant man, we would call "virtuous" in a woman.[6] The virtuous woman is known for her character and strength, and according to Proverbs 31:10, she is both rare and valuable.

The virtuous woman stands in complete contrast to the provocative, overtly sensual, "strange woman" of Proverbs, whose impudent sexuality is really nothing more than a public display of her insecurity. The strange woman uses her sexuality to attract men, which gives her a sense of worth or power. Fleeting as it is, she feels desirable, wanted.

Unfortunately, Satan has a much more pervasive advertising system than parents do. Television, movies, and video games often portray loose women as "sexually powerful," "progressive," or "taking charge of their own bodies." To make matters worse, popular culture icons in music and media take the strange-woman behavior to a whole new level, glorifying seduction as a way of life. The constant message our daughters receive is, "To be successful and happy, you must be highly desired as a sex object."

That's why our job as parents requires starting early. It involves helping our daughters to establish their security and sense of worth in something more substantial than the obsession of the nearest hormonal boy. "Who can find a wife of noble character? / For her value is far more than rubies" (Proverbs 31:10 NET). If we really believe that, then we must be diligent about our message:

YOUR WORTH IS TO BE FOUND
IN YOUR RELATIONSHIP WITH
THE LORD.

THEREFORE, CHOOSE TO BE
DESIRABLE FOR YOUR CHARACTER.

Interestingly, the character of a woman matters even to the most hypocritical of men. I remember sitting around with a group of fellow Marines when I was serving on Okinawa. Four of us were Christians, the other eight or nine were not. As we were talking about women (a common subject among Marines), someone asked, "What do you want most in a wife? What is the one thing that you would love to find in your wife more than any other?" Our unanimous answer was *purity*. I found that remarkable. Every man agreed that his first desire was a pure and virtuous woman. I silently thanked God for having already given me such a woman as my wife.

Now, keep in mind that the vast majority of the men in our group spent their weekends and their pay at the local brothels. The point of this should be clear. The provocative woman attracts only men who are interested in what she has to offer sexually—and usually nothing more than that. Even a hypocritical, impure man has no respect for the provocative woman. Once he has had his fun, he's gone. He has no interest in a long-term relationship.

So how do we prepare our daughters for virtue? In a practical sense, a girl's self-respect will guide almost every social decision she makes. If it is low, her choices will reflect it. If it is solidly grounded in her identity in Christ, her choices will reinforce her belief that she is a treasured creation of God, worthy of dignified treatment by others—including boys. So this is where we must focus our attention. We must establish her worth and teach her how to nurture it through her relationship with Jesus Christ. Her inherent value as God's creation should become the basis of our communication about clothing, flirting, dating, and purity.

A mother teaches by her example, by allowing her daughter to see inside her marriage. As a mother, share with your daughter your perspective on the role of self-worth and character in your dating life, your courtship with your husband, and your relationship today. Discuss how your relationship with Christ grounds your sense of dignity and how you present yourself. Do this regularly, which means setting aside significant, individual time for relaxed conversation. And most of all, show her how to be a woman of virtue through your dress, your interactions with men other than your husband, and by being appropriately, romantically affectionate with your husband, even in her presence.

Fathers help their daughters establish a healthy sense of self-worth in two primary ways. Daughters learn personal dignity first by watching how Dad treats Mom and second by how Dad treats them. As her father, you are the standard by which your daughter will judge all potential mates. Except in rare cases where her relationship with Mom is dysfunctional, she will choose nothing less than you. Set the standard high. Think of how you would want her husband to treat her, then treat your wife that way. Not only when you two are alone, but also in front of your daughter. Kids have a built-in authenticity detector. They know when it's a show and when it's for real.

Another important way a father can influence his daughter is through something I learned from my good friend and mentor Howard Hendricks and his wife, Jeanne. Before his daughter began to date, he made sure that she had already learned how a man should treat a woman. Dad took his daughter out on dates. Except for romance, it was a date in every respect. He asked her out, planned the evening, opened her doors, picked up the tab—everything you would expect a polite young man to do. This became a very sweet part of their relationship. And by the time she was old enough to go out on romantic dates, he had set the standard wonderfully high!

Having helped your daughter to lay a solid foundation, grounding her self-worth in Christ, you will find that discussions about clothing and flirting become more natural and less stressful. While shopping, you can guide your daughter using the question, "What would you like people to notice first about you?" If she genuinely feels good about who she is, she will answer, "My eyes," "My smile," or "My sense of humor." Those answers reflect the heart of a woman who wants to be attractive without being overtly sensual. When you see her flirting with a boy, you can help her understand the difference between conveying interest and manipulative behavior. If she knows herself and likes herself, the flirting will fade as she matures. But if you observe that attention from boys has become *too* important for your daughter, you have a basis for discussion.

I must warn you, though. If your daughter does not have this secure foundation in place, confronting her about provocative clothing and inappropriate sensuality will have no positive impact. It will lead only to arguments and further distance.

If, however, you can help her to build such a foundation, she will be a priceless and rare gift to her future husband. Proverbs 12:4 tells us that, "An excellent wife is the crown of her husband." The word *crown* is a metaphor for "honor" and "dignity." A wife's virtue testifies to the virtue of her husband. Other men will respect him more because his wife has excellent character. Furthermore, her character surrounds him with protection from impurity. A man feels deeply honored when a virtuous woman reserves her sexuality for him alone.

The Godly Woman

Perhaps you haven't thought of *godly* as being the opposite of *indiscreet*, so let me explain. The Hebrew term translated as "godly" is one of the most theologically rich words in all of the Old Testament. The noun *hesed* describes the Lord's patient, pursuing, steadfast, inexhaustible, covenant-keeping love. Various translations have chosen "pious," "righteous," "holy," "good," and "merciful," though none quite capture the full breadth of the term. *Hasid*, the adjective form, describes a person who is like God. In her character, a *hasid* woman is "God-ish," or "godly." [7] A godly person conforms most to the Hebrew idea of wisdom.

While the godly woman possesses a sharp, discerning mind, an indiscreet woman is shallow; she lacks depth and insight. Subtlety escapes her, and other than getting caught and paying consequences, she sees little value in doing right.

Though the word *hasid* never appears in Proverbs 31, the passage wonderfully describes the godly woman. It concludes with the words,

> Charm is deceitful and beauty is
>   fleeting,
> but a woman who fears the LORD will be
>   praised.
> Give her credit for what she has
>   accomplished,
> and let her works praise her in the city
>   gates. (Proverbs 31:30–31 NET)

The word *charm* means "a trait that fascinates, allures, or delights."[8] *Beauty* refers to one's external appearance. If a woman is not godly, charm conceals a hollow morality. If beauty is all she has, then she will have nothing when age mars her youthful features.

The godly woman, on the other hand, may be charming and beautiful because she has much more beneath the surface. She readily perceives that which is not obvious. She can hear beyond words that are spoken to read inflection and understand body language. And she can foresee the implications of her own actions and the actions of others. These skills give her wisdom to know how to handle difficult circumstances, particularly when people are involved.

Depth rarely comes naturally and never quickly; it must be cultivated. People don't necessarily grow deeper with age, although time is an essential part of becoming wise. Painful experiences can create the opportunity for growing deep, but they can be squandered. To cultivate godliness, the Lord gave little girls parents; you are essential to their development into godly women.

The process for cultivating godliness in girls is similar to the ways in which parents help establish a solid basis for self-worth. Nothing can replace a parent's involvement as both example and guide. I asked Cynthia how she came by her discretion. She remembered that, as a young girl, she and her mother would spend two or three hours every Saturday just talking about life. No lecturing. In fact, Cynthia probably did most of the talking. Her mom listened, asked questions, offered perspective, and helped her consider situations from several angles. They talked! And by the time she was a teenager, the idea of seeking her mother's counsel on a problem didn't seem like a big stretch. To this day she remembers those Saturday talks.

I have found two things that typically keep this process from happening. The first is a lack of adequate time. Nothing can shortcut the process of growing deep in godliness more than the absence of sufficient time. If all we have to offer is ten minutes a day, we cannot expect to have a significant influence on our daughters when they spend eight hours a day at school, four hours a day in front of the television or computer, an hour in front of a mirror, and who knows how long with friends. Setting aside several hours a week will demand sacrifice. Get used to the idea that rearing godly children requires sacrifice.

The second factor preventing relaxed, sustained dialogue is a reluctance on the part of parents to recognize and accept that their little girl is much more sophisticated than they want to believe. And while denial is certainly part of the equation, so is the fact that kids are exposed to so much more at an earlier age than their parents were when they were growing up. Their rapid advancement can be threatening to a parent who feels he or she can barely keep up as it is.

To cultivate depth, we have to be willing to go deeper than the world will take our daughters. We must keep the lines of communication open, authentic, safe, and free. That means we can't react in shock and dismay when our nine-year-old asks about birth control. (It's on television!) Be ready to give an answer that's more complete and more satisfying than she will get from her friends or a Web site. Far better that the information—even facts that you feel are beyond her years—come from you than from *anywhere* else.

A Word to the Battle-Weary

Now, I am enough of a realist to know that many reading this book already have a daughter in crisis. Maybe she's not even living with you anymore. Perhaps you sigh with regret, wishing you had done more or done things differently. But the years are gone, she is breaking your heart with a self-destructive lifestyle, and you fear that hers might be a hopeless case. I want to assure you of two things that may seem absurd from where you are.

First, *no matter how hardened she appears, your faithful love and your continued acceptance of her means everything to her.* That doesn't mean you accept all her choices or approve of everything about her behavior. But once you have made your case, you don't need to say anything more. She knows. If she is to be won, it will be through your tenderness and your empathy. In the meantime, she desperately wants to be connected to you, but for whatever reason, she cannot accept that possibility. Don't be fooled by her hostility.

Second, *where the Lord is involved, there's no such thing as a hopeless case.* To illustrate what I mean, I want to tell you a true story.

I know a woman who came from a very rough home. Most adults have not seen many of the things she experienced as a child. She received none of the training that I've been describing. Eventually, she escaped that situation, but she had already started down a destructive path. By the time she reached young womanhood, she made her living on the street . . . ultimately as a call girl in Las Vegas. For years, she sold her body for sex to one man after another. She lost count.

Through a marvelous chain of events, this young woman came to know Jesus Christ. And to her amazement, a young man fell deeply in love with her, accepted her completely, and married her. He studied for the ministry and became the pastor of a church not far from where I ministered for over twenty years in Fullerton, California. He and his wife enjoyed a marvelous ministry together for many years.

The Lord was able to win the heart of this sensual, cynical call girl and place her in His service alongside a wonderful, loving husband. As one of the Hebrew prophets once wrote in Joel 2:25, God restored "the years that the . . . locust [had] eaten." Today, she is a godly woman, a pastor's wife, and a loving mother.

He can do the same in any life.

Keep loving your daughter. Keep praying for her. Keep offering her an alternative to her destructive lifestyle. Keep living the truth, consistently modeling the character of Christ. And continue to believe that the Lord can do anything.

My Questions and Thoughts

My Questions and Thoughts

Chapter 4

Cultivating Wisdom

You Are Here

Self-esteem, self-acceptance, and self-worth are fundamental issues that affect a woman's life. These distinct yet interrelated qualities affect almost every attitude and drive almost every decision. Unfortunately, many popular child-rearing experts have confused the terms, lumping them all into the same concept, which they call "self-esteem." In addition to confusing the concepts, they have mistaken flattery for esteem-building, supposing that a constant barrage of praise and words of affirmation will help girls overcome the difficulties of childhood. Positive communication is helpful, even necessary. But children won't be fooled for long. They find it confusing to build self-worth and self-acceptance on something as flimsy as the power of positive thinking.

The Bible teaches that our self-worth, self-acceptance, and self-esteem must be built upon wisdom — in the Hebrew sense of the term:

> Biblical wisdom is both religious and practical. Stemming from the fear of the Lord . . . it branches out to touch all of life, as the extended commentary on wisdom in Proverbs indicates. Wisdom

takes insights gleaned from the knowledge of God's ways and applies them in the daily walk.[1]

To cultivate wisdom in our daughters is to give them a solid foundation in Christ and, therefore, a genuine reason to feel valuable and likeable, "not in haughtiness and pride, but in confidence and security. This is the concept of human worth intended by our Creator. . . . He formed us in His own image!"[2] As a young girl gains biblical wisdom, she finds personal worth and security in her relationship with the Lord. And because biblical wisdom dignifies His creatures, girls find greater confidence in themselves as they learn to live wisely.

What influences do you think have the greatest impact on your daughter's opinion of herself? Are these the influences you would choose for her? Why, or why not?

_____

_____

_____

_____

What influences do you think have the greatest impact on your daughter's understanding of womanhood? Again, are these the influences you would choose? Why, or why not?

_____

_____

_____

_____

If your daughter were to base her self-concept entirely upon your words and demeanor toward her, describe the person she would see.

_____

_____

_____

_____

How have you sought to cultivate wisdom in your daughter in the past?

_____

_____

_____

_____

Discovering the Way

As we seek to give our daughters a strong emotional foundation, we can build with one of two materials: vanity or wisdom. Essentially the choice is between sand and bedrock. In the 1980s, the chairman of the California state-commissioned task force on self-esteem and social responsibility wrote, "Virtually every social problem we have can be traced to people's lack of self-love: alcohol and drug abuse, teenage pregnancy, crime, child abuse, chronic welfare, dependency and poor educational performance."[3] The proposed remedy for this so-called plague of low self-esteem was to teach people how to love themselves.[4] However, rather than self-love—what the Bible calls "vanity"—we should provide a far better alternative: the cultivation of godly wisdom rooted in the fear of the Lord (Proverbs 9:10).

The concept of "self-esteem" continues to be a divisive issue, not only between the church and secular child-rearing experts but also within the body of Christ. As often happens, both sides of the debate have valid points that are misconstrued by the other because neither has adequately defined their terms. So in the interest of peace and clarity, let us agree on these definitions of *self-worth*, *self-acceptance*, and *self-esteem*.

Self-worth is the intrinsic value a person has as God's creation and the bearer of His image (Genesis 1:26–27). Nothing can add to or take away from this value because it comes from the Lord and no other. The degree to which your daughter recognizes her personal worth depends upon how deeply this truth permeates her thinking. It is the job of every parent to teach his or her children that they are God's much-loved creations whom He desires to know intimately. This is the foundation upon which everything they believe about themselves must be built.

Self-acceptance is the grace your daughter gives herself based on the grace she has received from Christ (Romans 3:23–24; 8:1). The forgiveness and acceptance of others is important, but it does not add to or detract from the fact that she is acceptable because Jesus Christ has accepted her (Romans 15:7). Thus, self-acceptance is the degree to which a person feels comfortable in her own skin and it's the reason she can forgive and accept others as they are.

Self-esteem is the degree to which a person likes herself or himself. While it is a valid need (self-loathing is not only unhealthy, it is contrary to the Word of God) it nevertheless derives from temporal factors, such as talent, aptitude, beauty, intelligence, success, relationships, and personal investment in the betterment of the world and other people. Very simply put, when Sally behaves well, does well in school, succeeds in some worthy endeavor, and receives genuine appreciation, she will feel good about herself.

These qualities are interrelated, but they are not the same. And when we confuse them or try to address one with another, emotional problems and destructive behavior will inevitably result. The primary job of parents is to develop these crucial qualities in their child from the very beginning of life. As your daughter understands her intrinsic value as God's creation and rests in the grace God offers through salvation in Christ, she will be ready to cultivate a healthy, humble self-esteem through her activities and interests. And if you are successful, your daughter will know herself, like herself, and be herself.

Self-Worth

Read Psalm 139:13–16.

According to Psalm 139:13, who is responsible for the design and formation of a child?

_____

_____

What is the psalmist's opinion of God's creation in verse 14?

_____

_____

_____

_____

Looking at verse 16, when did the Lord begin watching the child's development?

_____

_____

According to the same verse, what did the Lord do concerning the child's future?

_____

_____

Notice the words the psalmist used throughout this passage to speak of God's direct involvement in His creation: "You formed," "You wove," "I was made," "[I was] wrought." Then in verse 16, he wrote, "And in Your book were all written / The days that were ordained for me." Most English versions translate the Hebrew this way, but the literal meaning is more poetic. The Hebrew word used for "ordained" is _yasar_, which means "to form or fashion"—like what an artisan does when he or she molds clay, weaves tapestry, or carves wood. And we find the very same root word used in Genesis 2:7 when God "formed man of dust from the ground." [5]

The Lord fashioned both your daughter and her destiny.

If the Lord saw the child's destiny before she began to form, what does this suggest about her design?

_____

_____

_____

_____

Given this picture of God's intimate knowledge and involvement during pregnancy, what value do you think He places on your daughter?

_____

_____

_____

_____

A healthy sense of self-worth is the deeply held conviction that one deserves respect and honor for no other reason than she was made by God and bears His image. A girl who understands the true nature of her personal worth knows that her value is unconditional. While beauty, intelligence, talent, and even godliness are positive attributes that should be praised, they should neither add to nor detract from a girl's sense of self-worth.

Unfortunately, many people who suffer from a poor understanding of their personal worth compensate by highlighting or accentuating their beauty, intelligence, talent, or spirituality. They measure their personal worth by the respect or admiration they receive from others. In fact, they even seek to please God in this manner. Many Christians unconsciously think that greater godliness will cause God to value them more. The truth is, we cannot earn God's love and value for us. They have been unconditionally given.

The best and only remedy for someone who fails to recognize her own value is truth from Scripture. If she genuinely understands how much the Lord cherishes her and if she allows that truth to penetrate her heart, many of the battles she will face as a woman will have been won. In other words, her relationship with God is the beginning of wisdom.

Self-Acceptance

Self-acceptance is the degree to which a girl accepts her own imperfections—moral, physical, and otherwise—and her own failures. It is the degree to which she recognizes the free gift of God's grace she has already received and lives a grace-filled life.

Read Romans 8:1–2.

To whom does Paul's declaration apply?

_____

_____

What does he say about them?

_____

_____

_____

_____

_____

_____

What failures or flaws are excluded from this declaration?

_____

_____

_____

Read Romans 8:15–17.

Putting together what you learned from the previous passage with what you've gleaned from this one, on what conditions are those who are "in Christ" accepted as God's daughters and sons? (See also Romans 5:17–19.)

_____

_____

What place does fear of condemnation or rejection have in the lives of God's daughters and sons?

_____

_____

Paul explains one of the reasons that God's daughters and sons suffer pain or sorrow. Are they being punished or rejected? Why do they sometimes experience difficulty?

_____

_____

_____

_____

Read Romans 8:31–39.

Who is the final judge in the case of "the world versus the believer"?

_____

_____

Will God ever reject a believer? Why, or why not?

_____

_____

_____

What basis does anyone have to condemn or reject a daughter or son of God?

_____

_____

What basis does a person have to condemn or reject herself as a daughter of God?

_____

_____

The almighty, sovereign Judge of the universe has declared the believer "not guilty" by issuing a judicial pardon. Jesus Christ has paid the penalty for the sins of anyone who chooses to accept His free gift, leaving no room for anyone to condemn or reject the believer. This includes your daughter, if she has chosen to believe in Jesus Christ. What better reason for her to feel comfortable in her own skin? Christ is her Judge, and He has given her grace — unconditional, unmerited favor. The more this truth penetrates her soul, the less she will feel the need to gain the approval or acceptance of others.

Self-Esteem

Self-esteem is the measure of how much your daughter likes herself. It must be built upon a biblical understanding of self-worth and self-acceptance. Once a girl accepts her intrinsic worth as God's beloved creation and understands the grace she has received in Christ, her sense of inner well-being can be enhanced by the application of godly wisdom to temporal, conditional things, such as beauty, intelligence, talent, good behavior, and accomplishments.

A healthy self-esteem is neither too low nor too high—avoiding both narcissism and self-hate—and it must be fueled by godly wisdom. Proverbs 31:10–31 describes a wise and humble woman. She is our best example of feminine wisdom.

Wise Women Are Valued

In Proverbs 31:10, the word translated as "excellent" or "noble" is the same word used to describe a "mighty man of valor."[6] It is the feminine equivalent of a valiant knight whose honor and courage make him worthy of admiration. The outward expression may be different for women than for men, but the inner quality is the same.

Read Proverbs 31:10–11.

To what is the woman of excellence compared?

_____

_____

According to the passage, who considers her valuable? And why does this person do so?

_____

_____

_____

_____

How do you think a husband's response to his wife's positive qualities will affect her ability to like herself?

_____

_____

_____

_____

Wise Women Serve Others

Read the following verses. Who benefits from the wise woman's kindness, and what do they receive?

Proverbs 31:11–12 _____

_____

Proverbs 31:15 _____

_____

Proverbs 31:20 _____

_____

Proverbs 31:26–27 _____

_____

What do the verses say she gains in return?

_____

_____

_____

_____

How do you think a woman who serves others feels when she sees the results of her service? How is her self-esteem affected?

_____

_____

_____

_____

Wise Women Develop Their Talents

Read Proverbs 31:13, 19, 22, 24.

What craft does this particular wise woman develop?

_____

_____

_____

_____

How does her craft benefit the household and others?

_____

_____

_____

_____

How do you think a woman who develops her talents successfully feels about herself?

_____

_____

_____

_____

Wise Women Are Competent in Business and Money Matters

The writer of Proverbs describes the wise woman as being like a merchant ship, a welcome sight in the ancient world. Food, clothing, and other supplies were limited to what a local town could produce on its own, which could become quite boring. A merchant ship promised to bring what local growers and artisans could not produce as well as exciting and unusual goods from exotic, faraway places. To say that a woman is like a merchant ship is to suggest that her provision goes beyond the mundane to include things that are interesting, unusual, highly desired, or rare. The wise woman isn't satisfied with the bare minimum. She wants the very best for her family.

Read Proverbs 31:16–24. List the ways in which the wise woman spends her time.

_____

_____

_____

_____

What does the wise woman do with her handiwork?

_____

_____

_____

_____

How does the wise woman handle her money?

_____

_____

_____

_____

Describe the confidence level of a woman who works hard, invests well, and handles business wisely. Why do you think these things would influence the way she feels about herself?

_____

_____

_____

_____

Wise Women Choose to Make Godly Character Their Most Attractive Trait

From Proverbs 31:16–24, what attractive qualities do you see in the wise woman?

_____

_____

_____

_____

_____

How do the people around the wise woman view her? What characteristics do you think they honor or respect most? Why?

_____

_____

_____

_____

_____

Starting Your Journey

Self-Worth

In their early years, children assume that how we treat them reflects how God sees them. Here are some suggested ways to reinforce the truth of your daughter's value as a much-loved child of God and a bearer of His image.

First, from the very first day your daughter can hold a conversation, begin teaching her about God's unconditional love for her. Let her know that God created her the way He wanted and that He has special plans just for her. Give her a strong sense of security in a destiny that God controls.

Second, ask your daughter open-ended questions and get her talking. Set aside time to be alone with her, preferably doing something fun. Try a day at an amusement park (plenty of time standing in line) or an after-dinner trip to the ice-cream parlor. And encourage her to talk, to share her life with you. Here are some conversation starters:

- What famous person do you admire most?

- If you could live anywhere in the world, where would it be?

- If you could magically become an expert at something overnight, what would it be?

- What do you wish you could try but won't because you're afraid it won't work out?

- What is your greatest fear in life?

- What experience have you had that you wished wouldn't end?

Dreams are rarely realistic, but they are excellent windows to the inner person. Your purpose in freeing your daughter's imagination is not to plan a concrete future but to discover what motivates, intrigues, excites, or inspires her.

Third, reflect your positive observations to your daughter. As you see her do something well, casually mention it. As you take note of her strengths, tell her regularly what you admire about her and why. Affirm your belief that God has a special plan for her. Let her know how she makes you proud as a parent. Ask her questions about her interests and what she naturally feels competent doing.

Of course, discipline will be necessary from time to time. But discipline for negative behavior will have far greater impact when the majority of your daughter's experience with you is positive. Be deliberate about noticing what she does right and affirm it.

What are some specific ways you can guide your daughter toward wisdom using positive feedback?

_____

_____

_____

_____

_____

_____

_____

_____

Self-Acceptance

Carefully distinguish between true guilt and false guilt, both of which can lead to shame, the chief enemy of self-acceptance. Addressing the issues of guilt and shame begins with an honest assessment of your daughter's relationship with Jesus Christ.

To your knowledge, has your daughter accepted the free gift of eternal life through faith in Jesus Christ?
_____ Yes _____ No

If you answered no, the first and most important step is her salvation—accepting God's free gift of forgiveness and acceptance through Jesus Christ as full payment for her sin. Without Christ, she remains under the condemnation of her sin. As long as she feels she must pay her own penalty, she will not experience forgiveness and freedom from guilt and shame. Take time together to read "How to Begin a Relationship with God" at the end of this book.

If you answered yes, the best response to guilt and shame lies in understanding God's loving response to any and all of your daughter's sins. Review the following passages with her and highlight the main point of each one.

Matthew 11:28–30	God is compassionate.
1 John 1:9	God desires that we confess our sin.
Isaiah 1:18	God provides full and complete forgiveness.
1 John 2:1–2	God graciously recognizes our weakness in temptation, although it is His desire that we do not sin.

| Isaiah 43:25 | God no longer holds our sin against us; therefore, we are free from guilt and shame. |

For more information on how to respond to persistent guilt and shame, contact one of our seminary-trained pastors and counselors. See "We Are Here for You" on page 107 for contact information.

Self-Esteem

Pursuing a healthy view of self-worth and self-acceptance and finding a balanced self-esteem should not be confused with selfishness. One Christian counselor defines a healthy self-esteem as "the willingness to give up being the center of my world and accept myself as God's creation: lovable, valuable, capable, forgivable, and redeemable."[7] In other words, a young woman who knows her value in God's eyes and therefore likes herself has a greater ability to regard others as more important than herself. In order to assist your daughter in building a healthy self-esteem, consider the following suggestions.

First, without being too obvious, begin making a careful study of your daughter's natural abilities and interests. When you are out together, take note of what draws her attention. Plan a variety of outings, such as museums, concerts, craft fairs, the library, social events—anything that exposes her to a variety of interests. Try to determine what intrigues or excites her. You might even keep a journal of your observations. As you see a pattern emerge, find a way to explore those interests with her.

As you observe your daughter, what is she naturally good at?

_____

_____

_____

_____

_____

What tends to draw her interest, and what specific aspects of it attract her?

_____

_____

_____

_____

_____

When considering these natural talents and interests, how could you help your daughter recognize that she is loved and valued by God?

_____

_____

_____

_____

_____

Second, enable her. If she demonstrates an aptitude for something, suggest she explore it and find a way to help her. Purchase supplies, look for classes, find others who share her interest and have them explain why they enjoy what they do, learn more about it yourself and share your knowledge. If it eventually fizzles, let it drop without a single negative comment. But encourage her to keep exploring and experimenting.

Rearing a Wise Woman

For each of the characteristics of a wise woman, think of an activity that you and your daughter can do together that will allow her to see it in action. These suggestions may spark an idea or two. Be sure to list the activity you plan to pursue in the available space below each suggestion.

Wise Women Know Their Value

Share your understanding of how a woman should be treated, and arrange a date on which her dad or another trusted man can model it for her.

_____

_____

_____

_____

_____

_____

_____

_____

Wise Women Serve Others

Plan a day in which the two of you volunteer for a
ministry, preferably where you can directly interact with
the people served.

_____

_____

_____

_____

Wise Women Develop Their Talents

Find a way to include your daughter as you pursue one
of your own interests. She may not pick up on yours, but
she will benefit by seeing your enjoyment and growth.

_____

_____

_____

_____

Wise Women Are Competent in Business and Money Matters

Allow your daughter to make the mental connection
between work and the nice things you enjoy as a family.
Let the joys and benefits of hard work speak louder than
the drudgery or monotony. Insist that she start earning
money of her own as soon as possible, and celebrate her
accomplishments.

_____

_____

_____

_____

Wise Women Choose to Make Godly Character Their Most Attractive Trait

Your daughter needs to know you think she's pretty. Don't ignore this need as you encourage other attractive qualities in her. Help her keep the issue of physical appearance in perspective while faithfully affirming her beauty. Look for living examples of strong, feminine character and teach your daughter to admire them.

_____

_____

_____

_____

One rarely, if ever, gains wisdom without the deliberate involvement of an older, wiser person. And who better to cultivate wisdom in a daughter than her parents? You have an opportunity to help your daughter become wise, not by lecturing endlessly but by looking for teachable moments and becoming her ally when life presents challenges. In other words, through the wise application of affirmation and unconditional love, you can become the best example of God's loving instruction and acceptance.

What better way to affirm her worth as you and your daughter cultivate wisdom together?

My Questions and Thoughts

How to Begin a Relationship with God

The Bible is the most marvelous book in the world, and it is the true Life-Map that marks the path to God. This map not only tells us how to avoid pitfalls and how to navigate the sudden roadblocks in life, but it also reveals how to enjoy the journey to the fullest. How? It points us to God—our ultimate destination. It tells us how we can come to know God Himself. Let's look at four vital truths the Scripture reveals.

Our Spiritual Condition: Totally Corrupt

The first truth is rather personal. One look in the mirror of Scripture, and our human condition becomes painfully clear:

> There is none righteous, not even one;
> There is none who understands,
> There is none who seeks for God;
> All have turned aside, together they
>   have become useless;
> There is none who does good,
> There is not even one.
> (Romans 3:10–12)

We are all sinners through and through—totally depraved. Now, that doesn't mean we've committed every atrocity known to humankind. We're not as *bad* as we can be, just as *bad off* as we can be. Sin colors all of our thoughts, motives, words, and actions.

You still don't believe it? Look around. Everything around us bears the smudge marks of our sinful nature. Despite our best efforts to create a perfect world, crime statistics continue to soar, divorce rates keep climbing, and families keep crumbling.

Something has gone terribly wrong in our society and in ourselves—something deadly. Contrary to how the world would repackage it, "me-first" living doesn't equal rugged individuality and freedom; it equals death. As Paul said in his letter to the Romans, "The wages of sin is death" (Romans 6:23)—our spiritual and physical death that comes from God's righteous judgment of our sin, along with all of the emotional and practical effects of this separation that we experience on a daily basis. This brings us to the second truth: God's character.

God's Character: Infinitely Holy

How can a good and just God judge us for a sinful nature into which we were born? Our total depravity is only half the answer. The other half is God's infinite holiness.

The fact that we know things are not as they should be points us to a standard of goodness beyond ourselves. Our sense of injustice in life on this side of eternity implies a perfect standard of justice beyond our reality. That standard and source is God Himself. And God's standard of holiness contrasts starkly with our sinful condition.

Scripture says that "God is Light, and in Him there is no darkness at all" (1 John 1:5). He is absolutely holy, which creates a problem for us. If He is so pure, how can we who are so impure relate to Him?

Perhaps we could try being better people, try to tilt the balance in favor of our good deeds, or seek out methods for self-improvement. Throughout history, people have attempted to live up to God's standard by keeping the Ten Commandments or living by their own code of ethics. Unfortunately, no one can come close to satisfying the demands of God's law. Romans 3:20 says, "By the works of the Law no flesh will be justified in His sight; for through the Law comes the knowledge of sin."

Our Need: A Substitute

So here we are, sinners by nature and sinners by choice, trying to pull ourselves up by our own bootstraps to attain a relationship with our holy Creator. But every time we try, we fall flat on our faces. We can't live a good enough life to make up for our sin, because God's standard isn't "good enough"—it's *perfection*. And we can't make amends for the offense our sin has created without dying for it.

Who can get us out of this mess?

If someone could live perfectly, honoring God's law, and would bear sin's death penalty for us—in our place—then we would be saved from our predicament. But is there such a person? Thankfully, yes!

Meet your substitute—*Jesus Christ*. He is the One who took death's place for you!

> [God] made [Jesus Christ] who knew no sin to be sin on our behalf, so that we might become the righteousness of God in Him.
> (2 Corinthians 5:21)

God's Provision: A Savior

God rescued us by sending His Son, Jesus, to die on the cross for our sins (1 John 4:9–10). Jesus was fully human and fully divine (John 1:1, 18), a truth that ensures His understanding of our weaknesses, His power to forgive, and His ability to bridge the gap between God and us (Romans 5:6–11). In short, we are "justified as a gift by His grace through the redemption which is in Christ Jesus" (Romans 3:24). Two words in this verse bear further explanation: *justified* and *redemption*.

Justification is God's act of mercy, in which He declares believing sinners righteous while they are still in their sinning state. Justification doesn't mean that God *makes* us righteous, so that we never sin again, rather that He *declares* us righteous—much like a judge pardons a guilty criminal. Because Jesus took our sin upon Himself and suffered our judgment on the cross, God forgives our debt and proclaims us PARDONED.

Redemption is God's act of paying the ransom price to release us from our bondage to sin. Held hostage by Satan, we were shackled by the iron chains of sin and death. Like a loving parent whose child has been kidnapped, God willingly paid the ransom for you. And what a price He paid! He gave His only Son to bear our sins—past, present, and future. Jesus's death and resurrection broke our chains and set us free to become children of God (Romans 6:16–18, 22; Galatians 4:4–7).

Placing Your Faith in Christ

These four truths describe how God has provided a way to Himself through Jesus Christ. Because the price has been paid in full by God, we must respond to His free gift of eternal life in total faith and confidence in Him to save us. We must step forward into the relationship with God that He has prepared for us—not by doing good works or by being good people, but by coming to Him just as we are and accepting His justification and redemption by faith.

> For by grace you have been saved through faith; and that not of yourselves, it is the gift of God; not as a result of works, so that no one may boast. (Ephesians 2:8–9)

We accept God's gift of salvation simply by placing our faith in Christ alone for the forgiveness of our sins. Would you like to enter into a relationship with your Creator by trusting in Christ as your Savior? If so, here's a simple prayer you can use to express your faith:

Dear God,

I know that my sin has put a barrier between You and me. Thank You for sending Your Son, Jesus, to die in my place. I trust in Jesus alone to forgive my sins, and I accept His gift of eternal life. I ask Jesus to be my personal Savior and the Lord of my life. Thank You. In Jesus's name I pray, amen.

If you've prayed this prayer or one like it and you wish to find out more about knowing God and His plan for you in the Bible, contact us at Insight for Living. You can speak to one of our pastors or women's counselors on staff by calling (972) 473-5097. Or you can write us at the address below.

Pastoral Ministries Department
Insight for Living
Post Office Box 269000
Plano, Texas 75026-9000

The next time you study a road map, remember the One who created the perfect plan for your life, and remind yourself that you know Him personally. Rejoice in His indescribable gift!

Endnotes

Opening Quote

1. Alister E. McGrath, *The Journey: A Pilgrim in the Lands of the Spirit*, 1st ed. (New York: Doubleday, 2000), 21–22.

Chapter 1

1. R. Laird Harris, Gleason L. Archer, Jr., and Bruce K. Waltke, eds., *Theological Wordbook of the Old Testament*, vol. 1 (Chicago: Moody Press, 1980), 19–20.

2. James Swanson, *A Dictionary of Biblical Languages with Semantic Domains: Hebrew (Old Testament)*, electronic ed. (Oak Harbor, Wash.: Logos Research Systems, 1997), 222.

3. Harris, Archer, and Waltke, eds., *Theological Wordbook of the Old Testament*, vol. 1, 224.

4. Harris, Archer, and Waltke, eds., *Theological Wordbook of the Old Testament*, vol. 2, 579–80.

5. Harris, Archer, and Waltke, eds., *Theological Wordbook of the Old Testament*, vol. 1, 219–20.

6. James Strong, *The Exhaustive Concordance of the Bible: Showing Every Word of the Text of the Common English Version of the Canonical Books, and Every Occurrence of Each Word in Regular Order*, electronic ed. (Ontario: Woodside Bible Fellowship, 1996), 1566.

7. Harris, Archer, and Waltke, eds., *Theological Wordbook of the Old Testament*, vol. 2, 556–57.

8. Francis Brown, S. R. Driver, and Charles A. Briggs, eds., *A Hebrew and English Lexicon of the Old Testament* (London: Oxford University Press, 1968), 266.

9. Swanson, *A Dictionary of Biblical Languages with Semantic Domains: Hebrew (Old Testament)*, 6253.

10. Biblical Studies Press, *The NET Bible* (Dallas: Biblical Studies Press, 2003), www.Bible.org, Proverbs 11:22, n5.

Chapter 2

1. R. Laird Harris, Gleason L. Archer, Jr., and Bruce K. Waltke, eds., *Theological Wordbook of the Old Testament*, vol. 2 (Chicago: Moody Press, 1980), 742.

2. Harris, Archer, and Waltke, eds., *Theological Wordbook of the Old Testament*, vol. 1, 449–50.

3. Harris, Archer, and Waltke, eds., *Theological Wordbook of the Old Testament*, vol. 1, 19–20.

4. Harris, Archer, and Waltke, eds., *Theological Wordbook of the Old Testament*, vol. 2, 547–48.

5. Harris, Archer, and Waltke, eds., *Theological Wordbook of the Old Testament*, vol. 1, 479.

6. Harris, Archer, and Waltke, eds., *Theological Wordbook of the Old Testament*, vol. 2, 293–94.

Chapter 3

1. R. Laird Harris, Gleason L. Archer, Jr., and Bruce K. Waltke, eds., *Theological Wordbook of the Old Testament*, vol. 1 (Chicago: Moody Press, 1980), 282–83.

2. James Strong, *The New Strong's Exhaustive Concordance of the Bible* (Nashville: Thomas Nelson, 1990), see no. 7971.

3. Strong, *The New Strong's Exhaustive Concordance of the Bible*, see no. 2580.

4. Biblical Studies Press, *The NET Bible* (Dallas: Biblical Studies Press, 2003), www.Bible.org, Proverbs 31:26, n2.

5. Anne Ortlund, *Disciplines of the Beautiful Woman* (Waco, Tex.: Word Books, 1984), 127–28. All rights reserved. Used by permission.

6. Harris, Archer, and Waltke, eds., *Theological Wordbook of the Old Testament*, vol. 1, 271–72.

7. Harris, Archer, and Waltke, eds., *Theological Wordbook of the Old Testament*, vol. 1, 305–307.

8. *Merriam-Webster's Collegiate Dictionary*, 11th ed. (Springfield, Mass.: Merriam-Webster, 2005), see "charm."

Chapter 4

1. D. A. Hubbard, "Wisdom," in *New Bible Dictionary*, 2d ed., eds. J. D. Douglas and others (Downers Grove, Ill.: InterVarsity, 1982), 1256.

2. James Dobson, *Hide or Seek*, rev. ed. (Old Tappan, N.J.: Fleming H. Revell, 1979), 57.

3. Andrew Mecca, as quoted in "Promoting Self-Esteem," www.globalideasbank.org/BOV/BV-210.html, accessed January 15, 2004.

4. "The Self-Esteem Panacea," in *Counseling Insights: A Biblical Perspective on Caring for People* (Plano, Tex.: IFL Publishing House, forthcoming), 307.

5. R. Laird Harris, Gleason L. Archer, Jr., and Bruce K. Waltke, eds., *Theological Wordbook of the Old Testament*, vol. 1 (Chicago: Moody Press, 1980), 396.

6. Harris, Archer, and Waltke, eds., *Theological Wordbook of the Old Testament*, vol. 1, 271–72.

7. David E. Carlson, *Counseling and Self-Esteem*, vol. 13, Resources for Christian Counseling Series, gen. ed. Gary R. Collins (Dallas: Word Publishing, 1988), 21.

Resources for Probing Further

For further ideas on godly parenting, here are a few
resources we would like to recommend. Of course, we
cannot always endorse everything a writer or ministry
says, so we encourage you to approach these and all
other non-biblical resources with wisdom and
discernment.

Barna, George. *Revolutionary Parenting: What the
    Research Shows Really Works*. Wheaton, Ill.: Tyndale
    House, 2007.

Barna, George. *Transforming Children into Spiritual
    Champions*. Ventura, Calif.: Gospel Light, 2003.

Dobson, James. *The New Hide or Seek: Building Confidence
    in Your Child*. Grand Rapids: Baker, 2001.

Dobson, James. *Preparing for Adolescence: How to Survive
    the Coming Years of Change*. Ventura, Calif.: Gospel
    Light, 2005.

Etheridge, Shannon. *Preparing Your Daughter for Every
    Woman's Battle: Creative Conversations about
    Sexual and Emotional Integrity*. Colorado Springs:
    WaterBrook Press, 2005.

Feldhahn, Shaunti, and Lisa A. Rice. *For Young Women Only: What You Need to Know about How Guys Think.* Sisters, Ore.: Multnomah, 2006.

Jones, Stanton, and Brenna Jones. *How and When to Tell Your Kids About Sex: A Lifelong Approach to Shaping Your Child's Sexual Character.* Rev. ed. Colorado Springs: NavPress, 2007.

Kimmel, Tim. *Grace-Based Parenting.* Nashville: Thomas Nelson, 2005.

McDowell, Josh, and Bob Hostetler. *Beyond Belief to Convictions.* Wheaton, Ill.: Tyndale House, 2002.

Swindoll, Charles R. *Esther: A Woman of Strength and Dignity.* Nashville: Word Publishing, 1997.

Swindoll, Charles R. *Parenting: From Surviving to Thriving.* Nashville: W Publishing, 2006.

Wolgemuth, Robert. *She Calls Me Daddy.* Wheaton, Ill.: Tyndale House, 1999.